How to Unlock a Peaceful Mind

Strategies to Overcome Anxiety, Stress, and Negative Thoughts

ADAM WALKER

Table of Contents

Understanding Negative Thoughts — 1
- The Evolution of Childhood in the Digital Age — 2
- Statistics and Trends: Mapping the Rise of Youth Mental Illness — 5
- Implications of Digital Technologies — 9
- Insights and Implications — 11
- Definition of Negative Thoughts — 13
- Common Triggers of Negative Thinking — 18
- Impact on Mental Health — 21
- Introduction to Cognitive Distortions — 25
- Summarize the importance of identifying negative thoughts and their impacts while providing an overview of strategies to counteract them. — 29

Mindfulness for Mental Clarity — 33
- Basics of Mindfulness — 34
- Mindfulness Exercises — 37
- Connecting Mindfulness with CBT — 41
- Mindfulness for Stress Reduction — 46
- Readers will be equipped with mindfulness tools and strategies to mitigate stress, enhance mental clarity, and foster emotional well-being. — 49

Challenging Cognitive Distortions — 51
- Types of Cognitive Distortions — 52
- Recognizing Distorted Thinking in Yourself — 55
- Techniques to Challenge Distortions — 58

Case Study Examples	61
Understanding and applying techniques to challenge cognitive distortions can significantly improve mental well-being.	64
The Power of Cognitive Behavioral Therapy (CBT)	67
History and principles of CBT	68
How CBT works	72
Examples of successful CBT applications	75
CBT techniques for everyday use	80
Readers will gain a foundational understanding of CBT's history, principles, and evidence-based approach to tackling negative thought patterns.	84
Developing Emotional Resilience	87
What is emotional resilience?	88
Skills to develop resilience	91
Daily practices for strengthening resilience	94
Real-life applications of resilience techniques	97
Readers will gain an understanding of emotional resilience and its significance in fostering mental strength and well-being.	100
Creating Positive Thought Patterns	103
Strategies for Positive Thinking	104
Cognitive Restructuring	107
Replacing Negative Thoughts with Positive Ones	111
Daily Affirmations and Visualizations	114

    Readers will learn practical strategies, including mindfulness, cognitive restructuring, daily affirmations, and visualizations, to consistently implement positive thought patterns into their lives, fostering lasting positivity and well-being.   118

Reducing Anxiety and Stress   121
    Understanding Anxiety and Stress   122
    CBT Methods for Anxiety Management   124
    Mindfulness Methods for Stress Relief   126
    Exercises to Incorporate into Daily Routine   131
    Readers will have a toolbox of practical exercises to incorporate CBT and mindfulness into their daily routines, promoting sustained stress management and emotional well-being.   135

Achieving Lasting Happiness and Inner Peace   137
    Defining Lasting Happiness   138
    Role of Self-Awareness in Achieving Peace   142
    Sustaining Positive Mental Health Habits   146
    Future Steps for Continuous Improvement   150
    By following these strategies and incorporating the lessons learned, readers can work towards achieving sustainable happiness and inner peace in their lives.   154
    References   156

Chapter 1

Understanding Negative Thoughts

The transformation of childhood in the digital age is a phenomenon that cannot be overlooked. With the rapid advance of digital technologies, the landscape of childhood has undergone significant changes, manifesting through increased screen time and altered social interactions. The days when children spent hours playing outside have given way to an era where screens dominate their daily routines. This shift has profound implications for both physical health and cognitive development, reshaping how children grow and learn in the modern world.

This chapter delves into the multifaceted impact of digital technologies on today's youth. It explores how the prevalence of screens affects children's physical activities and mental well-being, highlighting the rise in health issues like obesity and sleep disturbances linked to sedentary behavior. Furthermore, the discussion extends to the cognitive realm, examining how early exposure to digital content influences developmental milestones and learning processes. Additionally, the chapter addresses the complex role of social media in shaping self-esteem and body image, alongside its contribution to increasing anxiety and depression rates among young people. Through comprehensive analysis and evidence-based insights, this chapter aims to provide a nuanced understanding of the digital age's implications on childhood and mental health, offering valuable perspectives for parents, educators, and policymakers seeking to navigate this evolving landscape responsibly.

The Evolution of Childhood in the Digital Age

The dawn of the digital age has changed childhood experiences fundamentally. Gone are the days when children spent their afternoons climbing trees and playing tag. Today, the allure of screens often surpasses that of the playground. This shift from outdoor play to screen-based entertainment has profound implications for physical and cognitive development.

Outdoor activities historically played a crucial role in childhood development, fostering motor skills, social interaction, and creativity. Children running around, engaging in imaginative play, and navigating social dynamics honed critical developmental milestones. However, the rise of screen time has begun to replace these invaluable experiences. Many children now spend a significant portion of their day engaged with digital devices, whether it be watching videos, playing games, or interacting on social media.

This transition raises concerns about the impact on their physical health. Sedentary behaviors associated with prolonged screen time can contribute to issues such as obesity, poor posture, and eye strain. The lack of physical activity also means fewer opportunities for children to develop coordination and strength. Additionally, excessive screen time has been linked to sleep disturbances, which further impacts overall well-being and development.

From a cognitive standpoint, early exposure to screens is altering developmental milestones. Studies suggest that the passive nature of some screen-based activities offers less stimulation than interactive, hands-on play. For example, stacking blocks or solving puzzles engages multiple senses and promotes problem-solving skills. In contrast, passively watching a video can limit a child's engagement and attention span. Moreover, constant exposure to rapid-fire stimuli on screens can affect concentration and memory retention.

While critics argue that digital devices impede traditional learning methods, it's worth noting that they also bring significant educational benefits. Digital technologies have made information more accessible than ever before. Educational apps and programs offer interactive, adaptive learning experiences tailored to individual needs. These tools can reinforce topics taught in school, provide supplemental exercises, and even track progress over time. Consequently, children who might struggle in conventional settings may find these digital aids particularly beneficial.

However, the integration of technology in education presents its own challenges. Teachers and parents must strike a balance between leveraging digital tools and ensuring that children remain engaged with more tactile, exploratory forms of learning. It's essential to monitor and manage screen time to maximize benefits and minimize potential drawbacks.

Recreational contexts have also been significantly reshaped by digital devices. Traditional toys and board games often give way to computer games, mobile apps, and online communities. While some digital games promote strategic thinking, teamwork, and creativity, others may encourage isolation or expose children to inappropriate content. The key lies in discerning which digital activities are constructive and setting boundaries accordingly.

Implementing guidelines for managing screen time in children is crucial to mitigate negative impacts. Recommendations include establishing 'tech-free' zones and times, encouraging regular breaks from screens, and promoting diverse recreational activities. Parents and educators should model balanced screen use, highlighting the importance of face-to-face interactions and outdoor play. By doing so, they help cultivate a healthy relationship with technology while preserving the essence of childhood.

Statistics and Trends: Mapping the Rise of Youth Mental Illness

The rise of digital technologies has drastically influenced the mental health landscape among young people. Over the past two decades, there has been a significant increase in anxiety, depression, and other mental health conditions in youth. Statistics have consistently shown that these issues are on the rise, with alarming trends indicating that more adolescents than ever are experiencing substantial mental distress. This shift cannot be examined without considering the expansion of the digital age and its impact on young minds.

Various studies highlight a strong correlation between the amount of time young people spend on digital devices and their reported levels of anxiety and depression. For instance, research has found that teenagers who spend more than three hours a day on electronic devices are more likely to experience high levels of anxiety and depressive symptoms. Moreover, the constant comparison with others facilitated by social media platforms often exacerbates these feelings, leading to a decline in self-esteem and overall mental well-being.

Comparative analyses of mental health indicators pre- and post-internet/social media ubiquity provide further insights into this phenomenon. Before the advent of widespread internet use and social media, rates of anxiety and depression among young people were significantly lower. However, as access to these technologies has become nearly universal, mental health conditions have surged. It is crucial to note that while digital connectivity offers numerous benefits, it also presents substantial risks, particularly for younger, more impressionable minds.

One major factor contributing to this rise is the impact of social media on self-esteem and body image among youth. Social media platforms often present an idealized version of reality, where users showcase only the most polished aspects of their lives. This constant exposure to seemingly perfect images can lead to unrealistic comparisons, resulting in feelings of inadequacy and diminished self-worth. Young people, who are still developing their identities, are especially vulnerable to these pressures.

To illustrate this, consider the phenomenon known as "social media-induced anxiety." Many young individuals report feeling pressured to maintain a certain online persona, striving for likes, comments, and shares. This pursuit of validation can become addictive, leading to an endless cycle of anxiety and dissatisfaction. Furthermore, cyberbullying, which is rampant on many social media platforms, compounds these issues, causing significant emotional trauma for victims.

It is important to understand that these mental health challenges are not just anecdotal but are supported by robust data. For example, a study conducted by the Pew Research Center found that 45% of teenagers reported feeling overwhelmed by all the drama on social media. Additionally, the same study revealed that 24% felt pressure to post content that would gain a lot of likes and comments, highlighting how social media platforms contribute to increased stress and anxiety.

Moreover, longitudinal studies tracking mental health trends over time have shown a direct link between the proliferation of digital technologies and escalating rates of mental illness. These studies indicate that the more integrated digital devices become in everyday life, the more prevalent mental health issues among youth appear to be. This relationship underscores the need for careful consideration of how much time young people spend in front of screens and what kind of content they are consuming.

The comparative analyses of mental health indicators before and after the advent of the internet and social media provide a stark contrast. In the era preceding digital dominance, children and adolescents were less likely to experience the intense scrutiny and peer pressure that characterize today's online interactions. They engaged more in face-to-face activities, which fostered stronger, more supportive social connections. The shift to a predominantly digital mode of interaction has disrupted these traditional forms of social support, leaving many young people feeling isolated despite being constantly connected.

Another critical aspect to consider is the pervasive nature of social media and its ability to shape perceptions of self and others. Platforms like Instagram, Snapchat, and TikTok frequently feature heavily edited photos and videos, setting unattainable standards for beauty and lifestyle. Young people, inundated with these idealized images, often struggle with body image issues and low self-esteem. This phenomenon is particularly pronounced among adolescent girls, who are bombarded with messages about physical appearance from a very young age.

There is also evidence suggesting that the passive consumption of social media content—spending hours scrolling through feeds without actively engaging—can lead to feelings of loneliness and exclusion. Unlike active participation, passive use does not foster meaningful connections or provide a sense of community, which are essential for mental well-being. Instead, it reinforces the idea that one's life does not measure up to the carefully curated lives of others, perpetuating a cycle of negative self-perception and emotional distress.

Mental health professionals have expressed growing concern over these trends, emphasizing the need for proactive measures to address the impact of digital technologies on youth mental health. Recommendations include promoting healthy digital habits, encouraging offline activities, and fostering open communication between parents and children about the realities of social media. Educators and policymakers likewise play a crucial role in shaping environments that prioritize mental well-being and teach young people about the responsible use of technology.

Implications of Digital Technologies

In the digital era, childhood has transformed dramatically. One of the stark manifestations of this shift is the increase in screen time among children. This phenomenon has far-reaching implications for childhood development and mental health. As screens—whether they be televisions, computers, tablets, or smartphones—become more prevalent, children spend less time engaging in physical activities. This reduction in physical activity can lead to various health issues, including obesity, cardiovascular problems, and metabolic disorders. Moreover, the lack of physical exercise affects not only a child's physical health but also their mental well-being. Physical activity is known to release endorphins, which help reduce stress and anxiety; thus, a sedentary lifestyle can contribute to increased feelings of depression and anxiety among youth.

Another critical aspect is the digital divide, which highlights the socioeconomic disparities in access to technology. While some children have constant access to the latest digital devices and high-speed internet, others may have limited or no access at all. This disparity creates an unequal playing field where children from lower-income families often lag behind in educational achievements and digital literacy. Such gaps can perpetuate existing inequalities, making it harder for disadvantaged children to achieve upward social mobility. The digital divide also affects how children socialize and learn, as those without adequate access miss out on valuable online learning opportunities and social interactions facilitated by digital platforms.

Despite these challenges, digital technologies do offer potential benefits, particularly in enhancing learning through interactive and adaptive tools. Educational software and applications can cater to various learning styles and paces, providing personalized education experiences that traditional methods may not offer. Interactive e-books, educational games, and virtual classrooms can make learning more engaging and effective. For instance, apps that teach coding through games can make complex concepts accessible to young learners, fostering a love for subjects that might otherwise seem daunting. Furthermore, digital tools can help children with special needs by offering tailored educational content and assistive technologies.

However, the integration of digital technologies into children's lives poses significant challenges for educators and parents. Managing children's screen time has become a pressing concern. Excessive screen time can affect sleep patterns, academic performance, and social skills. Establishing rules around screen use, such as setting time limits and ensuring screen-free times during meals and before bed, can help mitigate some of these issues. Educators and parents must strike a balance between leveraging the benefits of digital technology for learning and ensuring that children engage in offline activities essential for their overall development.

Insights and Implications

The chapter has provided a comprehensive examination of how digital technologies have transformed childhood, highlighting the shift from outdoor play to screen-based activities. This change has significant implications for both physical and cognitive development. The reduction in physical activity due to increased screen time has led to various health issues, such as obesity and poor posture, while also impacting mental well-being by contributing to anxiety and sleep disturbances. Additionally, early exposure to screens affects developmental milestones, as passive screen activities offer less stimulation compared to hands-on play which actively engages problem-solving skills and creativity.

Furthermore, the chapter delves into the correlation between digital device usage and the rise in mental health issues among youth. Studies indicate that extensive screen time, especially on social media, exacerbates feelings of anxiety and depression, fueled by constant comparisons and online personas. This trend underscores the importance of balancing digital engagement with traditional forms of learning and recreation to foster healthier childhood development. By addressing these challenges and implementing guidelines for managing screen time, parents, educators, and policymakers can navigate the digital landscape effectively, ensuring that the benefits of technology enhance rather than hinder the growth and well-being of future generations.

Understanding negative thoughts is crucial in our journey toward better mental health. Negative thoughts, though often dismissed as mere passing nuisances, can deeply affect our well-being and overall quality of life. They have the power to influence our moods, perceptions, and behaviors, creating a cycle that can be challenging to break. When we allow these thoughts to take root, they grow and spread, much like weeds in a garden, choking out positivity and growth. Recognizing their presence and understanding their nature is the first step towards addressing them effectively.

In this chapter, we delve into the multifaceted nature of negative thoughts and their significant impact on our daily lives. You will learn how to identify these detrimental thought patterns and recognize how past experiences and current environments contribute to their formation. We will explore practical techniques such as mindfulness and cognitive behavioral therapy (CBT) to help differentiate and manage negative thoughts. Additionally, we will discuss the physical and emotional symptoms that often accompany these thought patterns, emphasizing the importance of breaking free from the vicious cycle they create. By gaining a deeper understanding of negative thoughts, you can begin to transform your mindset and improve your overall mental well-being.

Definition of Negative Thoughts

Negative thoughts can have a profound impact on one's mental well-being, leading to increased levels of stress and anxiety. When negative thoughts dominate our minds, they can create a pervasive sense of unease that affects every aspect of our daily lives. For instance, dwelling on perceived failures or shortcomings can make us feel constantly stressed about our abilities and future prospects. This ongoing stress not only diminishes our overall quality of life but also hampers our ability to function effectively in both personal and professional settings.

Moreover, the relentless presence of negative thinking can escalate into chronic anxiety, where one's worry and fear become habitual responses. This chronic state of anxiety feeds itself, creating a vicious cycle that's hard to break free from. The impact of such negative thoughts is not just limited to mental suffering; it often manifests physically as well. People enduring high levels of stress and anxiety may experience symptoms like headaches, muscle tension, and fatigue. These physical symptoms further reinforce the negative thought patterns, making it even more challenging to escape the cycle.

Recognizing the toll that negative thoughts take on mental health is crucial in addressing and mitigating their effects. It's essential to acknowledge that these thoughts are not merely harmless musings but significant contributors to our overall distress. By understanding their impact, individuals can start taking steps toward managing and ultimately overcoming these negative patterns. Self-awareness is the first step toward change, enabling people to seek appropriate strategies and interventions that align with their needs.

Various factors contribute to the development of negative thought patterns, including past experiences and the current environment. Our past experiences, particularly those involving trauma or failure, can leave deep imprints on our psyche. These experiences shape how we perceive ourselves and our abilities, often skewing our outlook toward negativity. For instance, someone who faced repeated criticism during childhood might grow up internalizing those criticisms, which then influence their self-esteem and thought processes.

The current environment also plays a significant role in shaping our thoughts. High-stress environments, whether at work or home, can foster negative thinking by constantly exposing us to pressure and conflict. A toxic work culture, for instance, might lead to feelings of inadequacy and self-doubt, while a turbulent family life can breed feelings of insecurity and hopelessness. Both past and present circumstances intertwine to create a fertile ground for negative thoughts to take root and flourish.

Understanding these factors helps in identifying the sources of negative thinking, making it easier to address and counteract them. Awareness of one's history and environment allows for targeted interventions that can tackle the root causes of negative thoughts. By recognizing these contributing factors, individuals can adopt a more proactive approach to managing their mental health, seeking support and tools that address their unique situations.

To identify and differentiate negative thoughts from neutral or positive ones, techniques such as mindfulness and cognitive-behavioral therapy (CBT) are highly effective. Mindfulness involves paying careful attention to one's thoughts and feelings without judgment. By observing thoughts objectively, individuals can recognize when they are engaging in negative thinking patterns. This practice creates a mental space between the person and their thoughts, reducing the automatic impact of negativity.

Cognitive Behavioral Therapy, on the other hand, offers structured methods to challenge and reframe negative thoughts. In CBT, individuals learn to identify distorted thinking patterns, such as catastrophizing or overgeneralizing, and replace them with more balanced and realistic perspectives. For example, if someone tends to think "I'll never succeed," CBT encourages them to challenge this belief by examining the evidence and developing more constructive thoughts like "I have succeeded in the past, and I can do so again."

These techniques provide practical tools for individuals to gain control over their thought processes. By consistently practicing mindfulness and CBT, people can cultivate a habit of differentiating negative thoughts from neutral or positive ones. This skill is essential for breaking the cycle of negativity and fostering a healthier, more balanced mindset.

One practical guideline to follow when applying these techniques is to keep a thought journal. Documenting daily thoughts can help in identifying patterns and triggers of negativity. Reviewing these entries regularly allows individuals to spot recurring negative themes and apply CBT strategies to challenge them. This practice not only enhances self-awareness but also provides concrete steps towards transforming negative thoughts.

Real-life examples vividly illustrate the detrimental effects of negative thinking. Consider the case of public speaking anxiety – a common fear rooted in negative thought patterns. When approaching a public speaking event, many people experience overwhelming fear and apprehension. They might think, "I'm going to mess up," or "Everyone will judge me." These negative thoughts fuel anxiety, causing physical symptoms like sweating and trembling, which in turn reinforce the initial fears.

This negative spiral often sabotages performance, resulting in exactly what the individual feared: mistakes and perceived judgment. The aftermath confirms their negative beliefs, making future speaking events even more daunting. This cycle highlights how negative thoughts not only impair performance but also perpetuate themselves, creating lasting impacts on confidence and self-efficacy.

Another example can be seen in social interactions. Someone who harbors negative thoughts might believe they are unlikeable or socially awkward. This belief fosters anxiety in social settings, leading to behaviors like avoiding eye contact or speaking softly. These actions can be misinterpreted by others as disinterest or aloofness, reinforcing the individual's negative self-perception. The outcome is strained relationships and increased social isolation, demonstrating how negative thoughts directly influence one's social life.

Common Triggers of Negative Thinking

Identifying triggers that lead to negative thoughts is an essential step toward improved mental health. Internal triggers are one of the primary sources of these thoughts, often rooted in ingrained beliefs and attitudes developed over time. These beliefs may stem from childhood experiences or societal norms that have shaped how we perceive ourselves and the world around us. For example, if someone has been repeatedly told they aren't good enough, this belief can become deeply ingrained and trigger negative thoughts whenever they face a challenge.

Unresolved past traumas are another significant internal trigger for negative thinking. Traumatic events leave lasting emotional scars, which can resurface as negative thoughts during certain situations. For instance, someone who experienced bullying in school might still struggle with feelings of inadequacy or fear in social settings. Recognizing these past traumas is crucial for understanding why certain thoughts emerge and finding ways to address them constructively. Often, therapy or counseling can help individuals navigate these complex emotions and begin healing.

Additionally, our attitudes play a pivotal role in how we process our experiences. A pessimistic attitude can make even minor setbacks seem insurmountable, leading to a spiral of negative thoughts. Conversely, adopting a more positive outlook can mitigate the impact of these internal triggers, helping individuals maintain a balanced perspective. This doesn't mean ignoring problems but rather approaching them with a mindset geared towards finding solutions rather than fixating on failures.

External triggers also play a significant role in fostering negative thoughts. Job pressure, for example, is a common external stressor that can significantly affect mental well-being. Deadlines, demanding bosses, and high expectations can create an environment ripe for negative thinking. Constantly feeling overwhelmed by work responsibilities can lead to thoughts of inadequacy and self-doubt. It's important to recognize when job-related stress is contributing to negative thought patterns and take steps to manage it effectively, such as seeking support or setting healthy boundaries.

Conflicts in relationships are another potent source of external triggers. Arguments and misunderstandings with family, friends, or partners can lead to feelings of rejection, loneliness, and anger. These emotions can quickly translate into negative thoughts about oneself and one's worth. Open communication and conflict resolution skills are essential tools for mitigating the negative impact of relationship conflicts. By addressing issues head-on and working towards solutions, individuals can prevent these external stressors from dominating their mental landscape.

Media influence also cannot be overlooked as an external trigger for negative thoughts. The constant bombardment of news stories, social media posts, and advertisements can create an atmosphere of comparison, fear, and anxiety. Seeing others' seemingly perfect lives can fuel feelings of inadequacy and self-criticism. It's important to manage media consumption mindfully, recognizing its potential impact on mental health and setting limits to foster a more balanced and healthy mindset.

Recognizing patterns of recurring triggers is paramount in breaking the cycle of negative thoughts. One common pattern is the fear of failure, which can consistently lead to negative thought cycles. Those who experience this fear may find themselves avoiding new challenges or opportunities out of a deep-seated belief that they will not succeed. This avoidance reinforces negative thinking, making it harder to break free from the cycle. Identifying this pattern is the first step toward addressing it; individuals can then work on building confidence and resilience through gradual exposure to challenging situations.

Another pattern often seen is the tendency to catastrophize, or imagine the worst-case scenarios. For instance, if someone makes a mistake at work, they might immediately jump to thoughts of losing their job and being unable to support themselves. This type of thinking inflates minor issues into major crises, creating unnecessary stress and anxiety. Recognizing this pattern allows individuals to challenge their catastrophic thoughts, replacing them with more realistic and balanced perspectives.

Self-reflection exercises are invaluable for pinpointing personal triggers and initiating targeted interventions. One effective exercise involves keeping a thought journal, where individuals write down their negative thoughts and the circumstances surrounding them. Over time, patterns and triggers become evident, providing insights into what specifically prompts these thoughts. This practice encourages mindfulness and self-awareness, key components in managing negative thinking.

Mindful meditation is another powerful self-reflection tool that helps individuals observe their thoughts non-judgmentally. By spending a few minutes each day in quiet reflection, people can better understand their thought processes and recognize triggers without getting swept up in them. This practice creates a space between experiencing a trigger and reacting to it, allowing for more intentional responses rather than automatic negative reactions.

Impact on Mental Health

Negative thoughts have a profound impact on our mental well-being. They feed into psychological conditions like depression and anxiety, often making the symptoms worse. Imagine waking up every day with a cloud hanging over your head. That's what it feels like to carry negative thoughts. This mental weight can make even the simplest tasks seem overwhelming.

People dealing with depression and anxiety already have enough challenges. Add negative thinking into the mix, and it's like pouring fuel on a fire. Instead of focusing on ways to feel better, they might find themselves stuck in a loop of self-doubt and worry. Over time, this can make their mental health conditions harder to manage. Studies have shown that those who frequently engage in negative thinking are at a higher risk of having severe and long-lasting symptoms of depression and anxiety.

But it's not just about feeling sad or anxious. The consequences of negative thinking can spiral into other aspects of life. When someone's mind is constantly filled with negativity, they might start believing that there's no way out of their struggles. This mindset can lead to feelings of hopelessness, making it even more challenging to seek help or adopt positive coping strategies. Ultimately, recognizing how detrimental these thoughts can be is the first step toward finding healthier ways to think.

Our bodies are closely connected to our minds, and prolonged negative thinking can take a toll on physical health as well. It's not uncommon for people caught in cycles of negative thoughts to experience headaches, fatigue, and even a weakened immune response. These physical symptoms are the body's way of signaling distress caused by ongoing mental strain.

Headaches can be particularly debilitating, affecting one's ability to focus and complete daily tasks. Negative thinking often brings about tension and stress, which can manifest physically. Fatigue is another common issue, as constant worrying can drain energy levels, leaving individuals feeling exhausted both mentally and physically. This tiredness can perpetuate the cycle of negative thinking, as a lack of energy makes it harder to engage in activities that might improve mood.

A weakened immune response is perhaps one of the more concerning effects of prolonged negative thinking. Stress hormones like cortisol become elevated when someone is under constant mental strain, which can compromise the immune system. This makes it easier for illnesses to take hold and harder for the body to recover from them. Understanding the physical implications of negative thoughts underscores the importance of addressing them early on.

Relationships play a crucial role in our lives, providing support, love, and companionship. However, pervasive negative thinking can strain these connections, impacting both personal and professional relationships. When someone's mind is clouded with negativity, it becomes difficult to see the good in others and communicate effectively.

Negative thoughts can lead to misunderstandings and conflicts. For example, if someone believes they are unworthy of love or support, they might misinterpret a friend's actions as rejection or criticism. This can create unnecessary friction and distance between loved ones. In a professional setting, negative thinking can result in poor collaboration and decreased productivity, as individuals may doubt their abilities and struggle to work effectively with colleagues.

Furthermore, pervasive negative thinking can make it challenging to maintain healthy social interactions. Those caught in negative thought patterns might withdraw from social activities, fearing judgment or criticism. This isolation can further exacerbate feelings of loneliness and sadness. Building awareness around how negative thoughts affect relationships can encourage individuals to seek support and communicate more openly.

Breaking the cycle of negative thinking is essential for protecting mental health and overall well-being. Strategies like cognitive restructuring, mindfulness, and stress management can be incredibly helpful in mitigating negative thoughts and feeling more in control of one's mental state. Cognitive restructuring involves identifying and challenging irrational or harmful beliefs, replacing them with more balanced and realistic thoughts.

Mindfulness practices, such as meditation and deep breathing exercises, can also help individuals become more aware of their thought patterns without being overwhelmed by them. By observing their thoughts without judgment, people can develop a sense of detachment and reduce the intensity of negative thinking. This practice promotes a more relaxed and centered state of mind, making it easier to handle stress and anxiety.

Stress management techniques, including exercise, healthy eating, and adequate sleep, play a vital role in breaking the cycle of negative thinking. Physical activity releases endorphins, which are natural mood lifters, while a balanced diet and sufficient rest ensure that the body has the necessary resources to cope with stress. Combining these strategies creates a comprehensive approach to managing and reducing negative thoughts, ultimately leading to improved mental well-being.

Introduction to Cognitive Distortions

One common cognitive distortion associated with negative thinking is all-or-nothing thinking. This mindset leads individuals to view situations in extreme terms, often as either black or white, without recognizing any middle ground. For instance, a person might perceive their work performance as a complete success or a total failure, with no room for acknowledging partial achievement or progress. Such rigid thinking can contribute to feelings of frustration and inadequacy, as it fails to encompass the nuances and complexities of most real-life situations.

All-or-nothing thinking can be particularly damaging because it sets unrealistic standards and expectations. When individuals adopt this mindset, they tend to expect perfection in themselves and others. Any deviation from these high standards is seen as a total failure, resulting in a harsh self-critique or criticism of others. This binary viewpoint can lead to chronic dissatisfaction and stress, perpetuating a cycle of negative thoughts and emotions. Over time, this pattern can erode self-esteem and affect one's overall mental well-being.

To break free from all-or-nothing thinking, it's essential to practice recognizing and appreciating the middle ground. By acknowledging that most situations exist on a spectrum rather than at extremes, individuals can develop a more balanced and forgiving perspective. This shift helps reduce stress and fosters a healthier, more positive outlook on life. Embracing imperfection and celebrating small successes can significantly improve one's overall mental health.

Another prevalent cognitive distortion is catastrophizing, which involves predicting and magnifying worst-case scenarios. People who engage in catastrophizing often find themselves overwhelmed by fear and anxiety, as they constantly anticipate disastrous outcomes. For example, someone might assume that a minor mistake at work will lead to getting fired, or that a slight disagreement with a friend will result in the end of the relationship. This kind of thinking not only amplifies stress but also prevents individuals from enjoying the present moment.

Catastrophizing can create a state of perpetual worry, as the mind becomes fixated on potential negative futures instead of focusing on the present. This constant state of alertness can take a toll on both mental and physical health, leading to issues such as insomnia, headaches, and even depression. Moreover, when people are consumed by catastrophic thoughts, they may avoid taking risks or pursuing opportunities, further limiting their personal and professional growth.

To counteract catastrophizing, it's helpful to analyze the evidence behind these fears and challenge their validity. Asking questions like "What is the likelihood of this actually happening?" or "What steps can I take to prevent this outcome?" can provide a more realistic perspective. Additionally, practicing mindfulness and grounding techniques can help bring attention back to the present moment, reducing the grip of future-oriented anxieties.

Personalization is another cognitive distortion where individuals take excessive responsibility for events, blaming themselves for outcomes beyond their control. For example, if a project at work doesn't go as planned, someone prone to personalization might think it's entirely their fault, even if there were multiple factors involved. This habit of internalizing blame can lead to feelings of guilt, shame, and inadequacy, severely impacting self-esteem.

When people consistently personalize external events, they carry an undue burden of responsibility. This can lead to a distorted self-image where they see themselves as inherently flawed or incapable. Over time, this negative self-perception can stifle personal and professional development, as individuals may become afraid to initiate actions or make decisions for fear of failure. Furthermore, personalization can strain relationships, as it may lead to unnecessary conflicts and misunderstandings.

To address personalization, it's important to develop a more balanced view of responsibility. Recognizing that multiple factors contribute to any outcome allows individuals to distribute responsibility more fairly. It can be helpful to reflect on specific situations and identify external influences that played a role. By doing so, one can alleviate the tendency to self-blame and foster a healthier, more objective perspective on their contributions and limitations.

Labeling oneself or others negatively is another significant cognitive distortion that hinders growth and improvement. This occurs when individuals assign fixed, overarching labels based on a single event or characteristic. For instance, if someone makes a mistake, they might label themselves as "stupid" or "incompetent." Similarly, labeling others in negative terms can lead to rigid and unfair judgments that overlook the potential for change or growth.

Negative labeling creates a fixed mindset, where individuals believe that their abilities and qualities are static and unchangeable. This perception can prevent personal growth and perpetuate feelings of helplessness and defeat. When people apply negative labels to themselves, they may become less likely to take on new challenges or opportunities, fearing that their supposed deficiencies will be exposed. In relationships, labeling others negatively can lead to resentment and conflict.

Summarize the importance of identifying negative thoughts and their impacts while providing an overview of strategies to counteract them.

In this chapter, we have delved into how negative thoughts affect our minds and bodies, often trapping us in cycles of stress and anxiety. These thoughts are not just fleeting moments; they have a lasting impact, shaping our mental health and physical well-being. Recognizing the nature and influence of these negative patterns is an essential first step towards managing them.

We began by understanding what negative thoughts are and how they can make us feel overwhelmed with stress or even lead to chronic anxiety. For example, when someone continuously focuses on their perceived failures, it not only brings discomfort but also impacts their quality of life and efficiency. This constant stress can build up, turning into physical symptoms like headaches and muscle tension, which further perpetuate the cycle of negativity.

Identifying where these negative thoughts come from is equally important. Factors like past traumas or current stressful environments contribute significantly to developing these patterns. Negative experiences from childhood or high-stress workplaces can foster a mindset that is prone to pessimistic thinking. By recognizing these sources, we can start addressing them directly, breaking free from the grip of negativity.

We have also talked about techniques like mindfulness and Cognitive Behavioral Therapy (CBT) that can help distinguish negative thoughts from neutral or positive ones. Mindfulness allows individuals to observe their thoughts without judgment, creating a gap between themselves and their negative thinking. On the other hand, CBT provides structured methods to challenge and reframe these thoughts, turning a belief like "I'll never succeed" into something more constructive and balanced.

Keeping a thought journal is another practical guideline for managing negative thoughts. By documenting daily thoughts, people can identify recurring patterns and triggers, allowing them to apply CBT strategies effectively. Real-life examples demonstrated how negative thoughts could severely impact performance and social interactions, reinforcing the importance of tackling these thoughts head-on.

As we moved through the chapter, we also explored common triggers of negative thinking, both internal and external. Internal triggers, such as ingrained beliefs from childhood and unresolved traumas, play a significant role. External factors like job pressure or conflicts in relationships can also contribute to negative thought cycles. Recognizing these triggers helps pinpoint when and why negative thoughts arise, enabling more targeted interventions.

Understanding the broader impact of negative thinking on mental health highlighted its serious consequences. Persistent negative thoughts can worsen conditions like depression and anxiety, making everyday tasks seem insurmountable. Furthermore, these thoughts affect physical health, leading to headaches, fatigue, and even a weakened immune system. The connection between mind and body underscores the importance of addressing negative thoughts early on.

Relationships, too, suffer under the weight of negativity. Misunderstandings and conflicts are more likely when one's mind is clouded with negative thoughts. People may misinterpret actions as rejection or criticism, leading to strained personal and professional relationships. Building awareness around these effects can motivate individuals to seek support and communicate more openly, improving their interactions.

Ultimately, breaking the cycle of negative thinking is essential for better mental health. Techniques like cognitive restructuring and mindfulness can provide much-needed relief. Additionally, practicing stress management through exercise, healthy eating, and adequate sleep ensures the body has the resources to deal with stress effectively. Combining these strategies offers a comprehensive approach to reducing negative thoughts, fostering a healthier mindset.

The journey toward overcoming negative thinking starts with self-awareness and a willingness to change. By understanding the roots and impact of these thoughts, adopting effective strategies, and seeking support when needed, individuals can gradually transform their mindset. This transformation not only improves mental and physical health but also enhances overall life satisfaction. Embrace the tools and techniques discussed, and take the first steps towards a more positive, balanced, and fulfilling life.

Chapter 2

Mindfulness for Mental Clarity

Incorporating mindfulness practices into daily life can have a transformative effect on mental clarity and overall well-being. Mindfulness, at its core, involves being fully engaged and present in the moment without judgment or distraction. By focusing on the here and now, we can break free from the cycle of negative thinking that often clouds our minds. This chapter delves into various mindfulness techniques designed to help individuals reconnect with their inner selves and cultivate a sense of peace and clarity amidst life's challenges.

Throughout this chapter, you'll explore foundational concepts of mindfulness and learn practical exercises that can be seamlessly integrated into your routine. From Body Scan Meditation, which enhances body awareness and releases tension, to Mindful Breathing, which centers and calms the mind, these practices offer immediate and long-term benefits. Additionally, the connection between mindfulness and Cognitive Behavioral Therapy (CBT) will be examined, showing how combining these approaches can effectively challenge and reframe negative thought patterns. Whether you're taking mindful walks or practicing self-compassion, each technique is aimed at reducing stress and fostering a clearer, more positive mindset.

Basics of Mindfulness

Mindfulness is the practice of being fully present and aware of one's thoughts, feelings, and surroundings. This concept may seem simple, but its impact is profound. Practicing mindfulness involves paying attention to the moment without distraction or judgment. The goal is to experience life as it happens rather than getting lost in worries about the past or future. By doing so, individuals can begin to see their world more clearly and feel a sense of inner calm.

When we are mindful, we engage with our experiences in a deliberate way. Instead of moving through life on autopilot, we become active participants in each moment. This heightened awareness allows us to gain insight into our thought patterns and emotional responses. For example, noticing how our body feels when we're stressed helps us understand the connection between mind and body. This understanding is crucial for mental clarity, as it provides us with the tools to manage our reactions and make thoughtful decisions.

Furthermore, mindfulness encourages us to observe our thoughts and emotions without becoming entangled in them. Rather than reacting impulsively, we learn to pause and reflect. This practice can bring significant relief to those struggling with anxiety and stress, offering a powerful method to break free from cycles of negative thinking. Through regular mindfulness practice, we can start recognizing that our thoughts and emotions are transient, much like clouds passing through the sky.

Being in the present moment holds immense power in reducing anxiety and stress. Anxiety often stems from worrying about future events or dwelling on past mistakes. When we focus on the present, those worries lose their grip. Mindfulness teaches us to anchor ourselves in the here and now. Simple practices such as paying attention to our breath or the sensations in our body can ground us and provide immediate relief.

Moreover, engaging with the present moment helps diminish the constant chatter of the mind. This mental noise often contributes to heightened stress levels and makes it hard to think clearly. By cultivating mindfulness, we create space between ourselves and our anxious thoughts. This space allows us to view these thoughts more objectively and reduces their intensity. Over time, this reduction in mental clutter leads to greater mental clarity and peace.

Incorporating mindfulness into daily life doesn't require significant changes. Small, consistent efforts can make a substantial difference. Mindful activities like deep breathing exercises, walking in nature, or even savoring a meal can all serve as opportunities to practice being present. These moments help establish a more balanced state of mind, where stressors are less overwhelming, and clarity is more readily accessible.

Cultivating a non-judgmental and compassionate attitude towards oneself is another core aspect of mindfulness. Often, people struggling with anxiety and negative thoughts are harsh critics of themselves. Mindfulness encourages a shift from self-criticism to self-compassion. By observing our thoughts and feelings without judgment, we begin to treat ourselves with kindness and understanding.

This compassionate approach fosters emotional resilience. When we make mistakes or face challenges, instead of spiraling into self-blame, we can acknowledge our feelings and move forward constructively. Learning to forgive ourselves and accept our imperfections is essential for maintaining mental health. It allows us to confront difficult emotions without being overwhelmed by them, facilitating a path toward healing and growth.

Self-compassion also strengthens our relationships with others. When we are kind to ourselves, we are better equipped to extend that kindness to those around us. This improved interpersonal dynamic can enhance our overall well-being, creating a supportive environment that nurtures mental clarity. As we practice self-compassion, we build a foundation of positivity that permeates all aspects of our lives.

Fostering a deeper connection with inner thoughts and emotions is vital for enhanced self-awareness.

Mindfulness enables us to delve into our minds with curiosity rather than fear. By regularly tuning into our inner world, we can uncover underlying emotions and thought patterns that influence our behavior. This deeper understanding empowers us to make conscious choices aligned with our true selves.

For instance, recognizing recurring thoughts of inadequacy can open the door to addressing underlying insecurities. By bringing these thoughts to light, we can challenge and reframe them, ultimately reducing their impact on our mental state. This process requires patience and honesty, but the rewards are substantial. Greater self-awareness leads to increased confidence and a clearer sense of purpose.

Mindfulness also promotes emotional intelligence. As we become more attuned to our emotions, we can navigate them more effectively. We learn to identify and articulate our feelings, which enhances communication and reduces misunderstandings. This emotional literacy is invaluable in both personal and professional settings, contributing to more harmonious interactions and a more stable mental state.

Mindfulness Exercises

To enhance mental clarity and reduce negative thinking, incorporating specific mindfulness exercises can be remarkably effective. One such practice is Body Scan

Meditation. This guided technique involves focusing on sensations in different parts of the body to foster relaxation and heightened awareness. By systematically shifting attention from head to toe, practitioners become more attuned to their physical states, uncovering areas of tension or discomfort. This self-awareness helps in identifying stress points and releasing built-up tension, promoting an overall sense of calm.

Engaging in Body Scan Meditation also cultivates a deeper connection between the mind and body. For instance, by paying close attention to breathing patterns, muscle tightness, or unrecognized pain, individuals learn to listen to their body's subtle cues. This practice not only enhances physical relaxation but also sharpens mental clarity by eliminating distractions and grounding the mind in the present moment. Over time, this heightened bodily awareness contributes to reduced stress levels and clearer thinking.

Moreover, the regular practice of Body Scan Meditation encourages a non-judgmental attitude towards one's physical sensations. Instead of labeling feelings as "good" or "bad," individuals are taught to observe sensations without interpretation. This non-judgmental approach allows for a more compassionate and accepting mindset, which is crucial when dealing with anxiety and negative thought patterns. By fostering relaxation and body awareness, Body Scan Meditation creates a solid foundation for mental clarity and emotional well-being.

Another highly effective mindfulness exercise is Mindful Breathing. This simple yet profound technique involves paying close attention to each inhale and exhale, serving as a powerful tool to center and calm the mind. Practitioners are encouraged to notice the natural rhythm of their breath, feeling the air entering and leaving their bodies without trying to alter it. This focus on the breath acts as an anchor, pulling attention away from distracting thoughts and towards a state of calm presence.

Mindful Breathing is particularly useful for those struggling with anxiety and stress. By concentrating on the breath, individuals can interrupt cycles of negative thinking, creating space for more balanced and positive thoughts. In moments of high stress, taking a few minutes to practice mindful breathing can drastically reduce immediate anxiety levels, allowing for clearer decision-making and emotional responses. This practice serves as a quick and accessible tool to regain mental composure during challenges.

Incorporating Mindful Breathing into daily life also extends beyond formal meditation sessions. For example, pausing to take a few mindful breaths before starting a task or during a stressful meeting can reset one's mental state, enhancing focus and productivity. As mindfulness becomes integrated into everyday routines, the benefits of decreased stress and increased clarity become more pronounced. Thus, Mindful Breathing not only provides immediate relief from stress but also promotes long-term mental wellness and clarity.

Walking Meditation offers another practical way to engage both body and mind in the present moment. This mindfulness exercise involves walking slowly and deliberately, paying attention to each step and the sensations that arise. By focusing on the movement of the feet, the shifting of weight, and the rhythm of walking, individuals can cultivate a deep sense of presence. This practice transforms a mundane activity into an opportunity for mindfulness, grounding individuals in the here and now.

The practice of Walking Meditation highlights the connection between physical movement and mental clarity. By aligning the pace of walking with the breath, practitioners can create a harmonious flow that calms the mind and body. This rhythmic movement helps to release built-up tension and fosters a sense of ease. Engaging in Walking Meditation regularly can significantly reduce stress levels, making it easier to tackle everyday challenges with a clear and focused mind.

Walking Meditation can be seamlessly integrated into daily life, making it accessible to everyone. Whether walking to work, strolling through a park, or even moving around the house, these moments can be transformed into opportunities for mindfulness. By approaching walking as a meditative practice, individuals can bring a sense of gratitude and awareness to their everyday activities. This simple shift in perspective can have profound effects on mental clarity and overall well-being.

Emphasizing the importance of grounding oneself in the present moment through body awareness is integral to mindfulness practices. Being fully present means tuning into the current moment without dwelling on the past or worrying about the future. Grounding techniques, such as feeling the feet on the ground or noticing the sensation of sitting, help to anchor the mind in the now. This focused attention reduces the influence of negative thoughts and promotes a state of calm awareness.

Body awareness exercises facilitate this grounding process. By consciously directing attention to different parts of the body, individuals can break the cycle of unproductive thinking. For example, practicing mindfulness while washing dishes or feeling the warmth of the sun on the skin can serve as simple yet effective reminders to stay present. These small practices build resilience against stress and encourage a more balanced outlook on life.

Connecting Mindfulness with CBT

Exploring how mindfulness practices align with Cognitive Behavioral Therapy (CBT) can significantly enhance our ability to address negative thought patterns. One of the foundational practices in both mindfulness and CBT is the awareness of thought patterns. By practicing mindfulness, we learn to observe our thoughts without immediate judgment or reaction. This observational skill helps us identify recurring negative thinking. For example, if someone constantly thinks, "I'm not good enough," mindfulness allows them to notice this thought as it arises repeatedly.

Recognizing these patterns is the first step towards change, as it becomes clear how often and how deeply such thoughts affect one's mental state. By documenting these observations in a journal or simply noting them mentally, individuals can begin to see the connections between their thoughts and feelings. Mindfulness encourages us to be present with these thoughts without attaching to them, creating space for introspection and understanding.

Incorporating mindfulness into CBT involves systematically using this awareness to challenge and reframe cognitive distortions. CBT focuses on identifying and correcting distorted thinking patterns, such as black-and-white thinking or catastrophizing. Mindfulness aids in this process by bringing attention to these distortions as they occur. By being mindful, one can catch themselves during moments of distorted thinking and consciously choose to view the situation more realistically.

Linking mindfulness with CBT principles means using mindfulness techniques to become more aware of these cognitive distortions. When a person practices mindfulness regularly, they develop a heightened sense of when they are engaging in unhelpful thinking patterns. This awareness is crucial for recognizing distortions in real-time and helps in actively disputing those thoughts with evidence-based reasoning. For instance, someone might realize they are overgeneralizing events and, through mindfulness, remind themselves that one setback does not define future outcomes.

While mindfulness helps in recognizing these thought patterns, CBT provides the tools to reframe them. This combination ensures that individuals do not just become aware of their negative thoughts but also actively work on changing them. As a result, there is a more holistic approach to tackling negative thinking, combining awareness with actionable strategies.

Behavioral activation is another area where mindfulness can be seamlessly integrated with CBT. Behavioral activation focuses on encouraging individuals to engage in activities that they find rewarding or pleasurable, thereby improving their mood and reducing negative thoughts. Mindfulness supports this by helping individuals stay present and fully engage in these activities. When practicing behavioral activation, being mindful ensures that one appreciates each moment and experience.

For instance, during a mindful walk in the park, an individual pays close attention to the sights, sounds, and smells around them, making the activity more enriching. This mindfulness practice enhances the effectiveness of behavioral activation by making activities more immersive and fulfilling. It promotes a deeper connection with positive experiences, reducing the focus on negative thoughts.

Moreover, mindfulness can help in overcoming resistance to behavioral activation. Often, people struggling with anxiety or depression may feel reluctant to engage in activities. Mindfulness teaches us to acknowledge these feelings without judgment and proceed with action regardless. This mindful approach can motivate individuals to participate in activities even when they initially don't feel like it, leveraging the power of small positive actions to create significant changes over time.

Self-compassion practice is another critical aspect of integrating mindfulness with CBT. Self-compassion involves treating oneself with kindness and understanding during times of suffering or perceived inadequacy. By incorporating mindfulness-based self-compassion techniques, individuals learn to recognize and soothe their emotional pain. This practice is particularly beneficial when addressing negative self-talk, a common issue in many mental health struggles.

For example, when someone faces a failure, instead of succumbing to negative self-talk like "I'm a failure," mindfulness encourages them to observe their thoughts and feelings non-judgmentally. They can then apply self-compassion by acknowledging their discomfort and responding with kindness, saying, "It's okay to feel this way; everyone makes mistakes." This shift from self-criticism to self-kindness fosters emotional regulation and resilience.

Combining mindfulness with self-compassion in CBT creates a supportive inner dialogue, essential for long-term mental well-being. It reduces the intensity of negative emotions and promotes a balanced perspective on personal challenges. Over time, this practice builds a robust foundation of self-acceptance and empathy, crucial for sustaining mental clarity and reducing negative thinking.

In conclusion, aligning mindfulness practices with the principles of Cognitive Behavioral Therapy offers a comprehensive approach to addressing negative thought patterns. Through awareness of thought patterns, we learn to observe and identify recurring negative thoughts. Linking mindfulness to CBT concepts enables recognition and correction of cognitive distortions. Behavioral activation, enhanced by mindfulness, stimulates positive behavior change and enriches experiences. Finally, mindfulness-based self-compassion techniques promote emotional regulation and self-kindness, vital for overcoming negative self-talk and fostering mental clarity.

Mindfulness for Stress Reduction

Understanding how mindfulness can play a role in reducing stress and enhancing mental clarity is essential in our fast-paced world. Stress response awareness is the first step in this journey. Through mindfulness, individuals can learn to identify their stress triggers and understand how their bodies react. This heightened awareness allows for early intervention, which can prevent stress from escalating.

Imagine you're at work, and an unexpected deadline is suddenly upon you. By practicing mindfulness, you can recognize the initial signs of stress—a faster heartbeat, shallow breathing, or muscle tension. Rather than allowing these symptoms to spiral out of control, mindfulness helps you pause and address them right away.

Guidelines can be helpful here. Start by setting aside just five minutes each day for a simple mindfulness practice like focusing on your breath. Notice where you feel tension in your body. Over time, this practice will help you become more attuned to your stress responses, making it easier to manage them in real-time.

Utilizing mindfulness to recognize signs of stress and prevent escalation is crucial. Once you are aware of your stress responses, mindfulness can guide you through managing them effectively. Instead of getting swept away by stress, you can use mindful breathing or grounding techniques to regain control.

Let's say you're stuck in traffic and running late for a meeting. Instead of letting anxiety take over, you might focus on your breath, noticing each inhale and exhale. This brings you back to the present moment and reduces the emotional impact of the situation.

Mindfulness trains your mind to respond rather than react. Over time, this proactive approach can significantly reduce overall stress levels, fostering a sense of calm and control even in challenging situations.

Introducing structured Mindfulness-Based Stress Reduction (MBSR) techniques offers a systematic way to combat stress and promote relaxation. Developed by Jon Kabat-Zinn, MBSR includes practices such as body scan meditation, mindful breathing, and yoga. These techniques are designed to help individuals connect with the present moment, reducing the impact of stress on their minds and bodies.

Consider adopting a regular MBSR routine. For example, dedicating twenty minutes each morning to mindful yoga or a body scan can set a positive tone for the day. Not only does this practice alleviate stress, but it also enhances overall well-being.

The beauty of MBSR is its flexibility. Whether you have five minutes or an hour, you can choose a practice that fits into your schedule. Consistency is key; the more regularly you engage with these techniques, the more profound their effects on your stress levels and mental clarity.

Moving forward, implementing mindful coping strategies during stressful moments offers immediate relief. When faced with a challenging situation, using mindfulness techniques can transform your reaction. Techniques such as mindful breathing, progressive muscle relaxation, or guided imagery can bring an instant sense of calm.

Picture yourself at a family gathering that's becoming tense. Rather than engaging in the conflict, you might take a moment to focus on your breathing. This pause can provide the clarity needed to approach the situation calmly and constructively.

Mindful coping strategies empower you to handle stress in the moment. By incorporating these techniques into your daily life, you create a toolkit for navigating stressful situations with grace and resilience.

Incorporating mindfulness into everyday activities further promotes mental clarity and stress reduction. Simple practices like mindful eating, walking, or even washing dishes can reinforce a state of mindfulness throughout your day. The goal is to remain present and fully engage with whatever task you're performing.

Consider starting your day with a mindful breakfast, paying attention to the colors, textures, and flavors of your food. Throughout the day, take brief mindful breaks to check in with your body and breath. These small moments of mindfulness accumulate, creating a more grounded and clear-headed state of being.

Readers will be equipped with mindfulness tools and strategies to mitigate stress, enhance mental clarity, and foster emotional well-being.

This chapter has delved into the profound impact of mindfulness practices on achieving clarity and reducing negative thinking. We explored how being present in each moment can shift our perspective, allowing us to engage with life more consciously. By observing our thoughts and emotions without judgment, we gain insights into our inner world, fostering a sense of calm and emotional resilience.

As mentioned at the outset, mindfulness isn't about emptying the mind but about becoming aware of our experiences as they unfold. Through regular practice, such as mindful breathing or body scan meditation, we establish a deeper connection between mind and body.

This awareness helps break the cycle of unproductive thoughts and brings immediate stress relief. The results are transformative: reduced anxiety, clearer thinking, and a balanced mental state.

However, it's natural for some readers to wonder whether these practices can fit into their busy lives. While it might seem challenging at first, incorporating small, consistent efforts into daily routines can yield significant benefits. Even brief moments of mindfulness —like savoring a meal or taking a few mindful breaths— can make a difference. The journey requires patience and commitment, but the rewards of increased mental clarity and reduced stress are well worth the effort.

Mindfulness offers benefits on a broader scale too. As we become kinder to ourselves, we positively influence our relationships with others. A compassionate attitude towards oneself fosters empathy and better interpersonal connections, creating a supportive environment that nurtures mental well-being.

In essence, cultivating mindfulness is a powerful tool for anyone looking to improve their mental health. By embracing the present moment, we can navigate life's challenges with grace and composure. Mindfulness doesn't promise a life free of difficulties but equips us with the resilience to face them thoughtfully. So, let's embrace this practice and see where it leads us, one mindful moment at a time.

Chapter 3

Challenging Cognitive Distortions

Challenging cognitive distortions is like untangling a knot in your thoughts. Have you ever caught yourself thinking in extremes, like seeing things as either fantastic or disastrous? You might be engaging in all-or-nothing thinking. Or maybe you've found yourself predicting the worst possible outcomes, even when they're not likely to happen. This habit is known as catastrophizing. Recognizing these patterns can be the first step towards freeing your mind from unnecessary stress and anxiety.

In this chapter, we'll dive into various common cognitive distortions and how they can affect your mental well-being. You'll learn about different examples of distorted thinking, such as personalization, where individuals take on responsibility for events outside their control, and filtering, which involves focusing solely on negative details while ignoring positives. We'll guide you through practical techniques to identify and challenge these distortions, encouraging you to shift your perspective toward a more balanced and realistic outlook. By understanding and addressing these thought patterns, you can cultivate a healthier, more positive mindset.

Types of Cognitive Distortions

Understanding how our thoughts can become distorted and affect our mental well-being is crucial. Cognitive distortions are patterns of thinking that can lead to negative emotions and behaviors. One common distortion is All-or-nothing Thinking. This is when we see things in black-and-white terms, without considering any gray areas. For example, if someone gets a B on a test, they might think, "I'm a failure because I didn't get an A." This type of thinking can create unnecessary stress and disappointment.

Recognizing all-or-nothing thinking is the first step to overcoming it. Instead of seeing things as entirely good or bad, try to find the middle ground. Life is rarely so clear-cut, and most situations fall somewhere in between. For instance, getting a B on a test is far from failing and still demonstrates a good understanding of the material. Shifting your perspective in this way can help alleviate feelings of inadequacy and foster a more balanced outlook.

To challenge all-or-nothing thinking, ask yourself questions that encourage nuance. Consider what aspects of the situation went well and where there's room for improvement. Reflect on whether your expectations were realistic and if this one event defines your overall abilities. By doing so, you can begin to see the broader picture and reduce the stress that comes with rigid, binary thinking.

Another common cognitive distortion is Catastrophizing. This involves magnifying the negative aspects of a situation and predicting the worst possible outcome. For example, if someone makes a small mistake at work, they might think, "I'll probably be fired for this." This pattern of thinking can lead to excessive anxiety and fear.

Realizing when you're catastrophizing can help you put things into perspective. Take a moment to evaluate the likelihood of the worst-case scenario actually happening. Often, our fears are exaggerated and not reflective of reality. By challenging these thoughts, you can reduce unnecessary worry.

An effective way to counteract catastrophizing is to consider the best-case and most likely scenarios alongside the worst-case one. This balanced approach can help you see that the actual outcome is probably somewhere in between the extremes. This method can significantly decrease the level of anxiety associated with anticipating disastrous consequences.

Personalization is another form of cognitive distortion. This occurs when you take responsibility for events that are not entirely under your control. For example, if a friend is upset, you might automatically assume it's because of something you did. This kind of thinking can lead to feelings of guilt and low self-esteem.

Understanding that you are not responsible for everything that happens around you can be liberating. It's important to differentiate between what is within your sphere of influence and what is not. Not everything revolves around you, and many factors contribute to any given situation.

By letting go of unnecessary guilt or blame, you can improve your self-esteem. Remind yourself that other people have their own lives, choices, and reasons for their actions. Their emotions and reactions are not always a reflection of your behavior. This realization can help you build healthier relationships and a stronger sense of self-worth.

Filtering is the tendency to focus solely on negative details while ignoring positive aspects of a situation. For instance, you may receive multiple compliments but fixate on one piece of criticism. This can skew your perception and leave you feeling incomplete or unappreciated.

Balancing your perspective by acknowledging both positive and negative elements is essential for maintaining well-being. Make an effort to consciously recognize and appreciate the good things in your life, no matter how small they may seem. This shift in focus can enhance your overall happiness.

Practicing gratitude can help you combat filtering. Keeping a journal where you jot down positive experiences and achievements can serve as a reminder of the good things that happen every day. Over time, this practice can help train your mind to notice and value positive moments, reducing the impact of negative ones.

Recognizing Distorted Thinking in Yourself

Identifying when your thoughts are distorted and learning to observe them objectively is crucial for improving mental health and developing a positive mindset. One effective method to achieve this is through mindfulness practice. By cultivating awareness of your thoughts without judgment, you can begin to see them more clearly and understand their impact on your emotions and behaviors. Mindfulness involves staying present in the moment and observing your thoughts as they arise, rather than getting carried away by them.

To start practicing mindfulness, find a quiet space where you can sit comfortably without distractions. Close your eyes and take a few deep breaths, focusing on the sensation of your breath entering and leaving your body. As thoughts come to mind, simply notice them without labeling them as good or bad. Let these thoughts pass like clouds in the sky, returning your focus to your breathing each time you get distracted. Over time, this practice can help you become more aware of your thought patterns and how they affect your mood and actions.

Another essential aspect of identifying cognitive distortions is recognizing how your emotions influence your thought patterns. Emotional awareness allows you to understand the connection between what you feel and how you think, providing insight into distorted thinking. For example, if you often feel anxious, you might notice that your thoughts tend to be overly negative or self-critical. By acknowledging these emotions and their impact, you can start to challenge and reframe your distorted thoughts.

One way to cultivate emotional awareness is by paying attention to your physical sensations and reactions throughout the day. Notice how your body feels during different emotional states, such as tension in your shoulders when you're stressed or a sense of lightness when you're happy. Identifying these physical cues can help you become more attuned to your emotional experiences and how they shape your thoughts. Additionally, taking a few moments each day to reflect on your emotional state can further enhance this awareness, making it easier to pinpoint when your thoughts are being influenced by strong emotions.

Journaling is a powerful tool for analyzing and challenging your thoughts. Writing down your thoughts helps externalize them, making it easier to identify patterns and distortions. Start by setting aside some time each day to jot down whatever is on your mind. Don't worry about grammar or structure; the goal is to capture your thoughts as they are. Once you've written them down, review your entries to look for recurring themes or negative patterns.

A thought journal can reveal underlying issues that contribute to distorted thinking, such as unrealistic expectations or an excessive need for approval. By identifying these patterns, you can begin to question their validity and consider alternative perspectives. For instance, if you notice a tendency to catastrophize situations, remind yourself that things often turn out better than expected. Reframing your thoughts in this way can reduce anxiety and promote a more balanced outlook.

Keeping a thought journal not only helps in identifying distortions but also provides a record of your progress over time. As you continue to document and analyze your thoughts, you'll likely see a shift in how you perceive and respond to various situations. This ongoing practice reinforces the process of challenging cognitive distortions and supports the development of healthier thought patterns.

Techniques to Challenge Distortions

Challenging cognitive distortions starts with evaluating evidence. When we examine the facts supporting our negative thoughts, we often find that our beliefs are based on assumptions rather than realities. An example of this could be feeling unworthy because you made a mistake at work. To challenge this thought, you would list all your accomplishments and positive feedback received in your job. This helps to create a balanced view, showcasing that one mistake doesn't define your overall worth.

Another practical strategy is to write down your negative thoughts and then ask yourself a series of questions about them. Are these thoughts based on emotions or facts? What evidence is there for and against these thoughts? For instance, if you think, "I'll never be good at anything," you can counter this by listing past successes, proving that this statement isn't true. This method allows you to take a step back and view your thoughts more objectively.

Lastly, comparing your thoughts to reality can highlight any discrepancies. For instance, if you're convinced that everyone dislikes you, try to recall recent interactions with people. Were they genuinely negative, or is it possible that you're interpreting neutral or even positive interactions as negative? This evidence-based approach helps to dismantle distorted thinking patterns efficiently.

Next, we look at cognitive restructuring. This involves replacing negative thoughts with more rational and positive alternatives. Cognitive restructuring begins with identifying the irrational beliefs underlying your distortions. If you believe that making one mistake means you're a failure, recognize that this is an extreme and untrue belief. The goal here is to find a more balanced perspective, such as acknowledging that everyone makes mistakes and they don't define someone's worth or abilities.

Engaging in positive self-talk can also help to restructure negative thoughts. For example, if you catch yourself thinking, "I can't do this," counter it with, "This is challenging, but I can learn and improve." Over time, practicing positive self-talk can gradually shift your mindset towards a healthier direction, helping you build resilience against stress and anxiety.

Visualization techniques are another useful tool in cognitive restructuring. Imagine how you would advise a friend dealing with the same negative thoughts. Often, we are kinder and more rational when helping others. Apply that advice to yourself and visualize acting on those positive thoughts. This not only helps in reframing your thoughts but also builds emotional strength.

Reality testing involves testing the accuracy of your perceptions through objective observations. This might involve looking at situations from different angles. If you think someone acted rudely because they don't like you, consider other explanations. Maybe they were having a bad day or were preoccupied with something else. By testing these alternative hypotheses, you can reduce the impact of your initial negative interpretation.

Another aspect of reality testing is seeking out corroborating or conflicting evidence. For example, if you feel you performed poorly in a meeting, ask colleagues for their honest feedback. You might discover that your performance wasn't as negative as you perceived. Gathering this kind of information provides a clearer picture of reality, helping you to correct any misinterpretations.

Finally, engaging in behaviors that contradict your negative thoughts can be enlightening. If you believe you're not sociable, try attending social gatherings and observe how people respond to you. Often, you'll find your negative beliefs are unfounded, which helps to recalibrate your perceptions closer to reality.

Seeking feedback from others can offer crucial insights into your distorted thoughts. Friends, family, and colleagues can provide perspectives that you might not have considered. They might see strengths and qualities in you that you overlook due to your negative thought patterns. Sharing your thoughts and feelings with trusted individuals can provide the validation or constructive criticism needed to challenge and reframe your views.

Additionally, professional guidance from a therapist can be invaluable. Therapists are trained to identify cognitive distortions and teach you techniques for challenging them. Therapy offers a safe space to explore your thoughts deeply and develop personalized strategies for managing them.

Peer support groups can also offer a unique form of feedback. Hearing about others' experiences and how they've dealt with similar issues can be reassuring and educational. It's helpful to know that you're not alone in your struggles and to learn practical tips from people who understand what you're going through.

Case Study Examples

When dealing with cognitive distortions, it helps to see real-world examples of how these thinking patterns can be transformed. Take, for instance, Anna's story. Anna was stuck in all-or-nothing thinking, perceiving her efforts as either complete successes or total failures. This mindset caused her significant stress and anxiety, particularly at work where every critique felt like a testament to her incompetence. Through counseling and self-awareness exercises, she learned to recognize the gray areas between absolute success and failure.

Anna's journey began with understanding that her rigid thinking was not based on reality but rather on a distorted view of her abilities. She started by listing instances where her all-or-nothing thoughts emerged. For example, if a project didn't go perfectly, instead of labeling it a failure, she would identify what went well and areas for improvement. She used cognitive restructuring techniques, questioning the validity of her extreme perspectives and experimenting with more balanced thoughts.

The steps taken to challenge and reframe extreme perspectives include several practical strategies. First, it's crucial to identify and acknowledge the distorted thought. Anna did this by journaling her thoughts and noting when she swung to extremes. Next, she compared these thoughts against evidence from her past experiences. This often involved writing down factual counterpoints to her negative thoughts, highlighting moments where things went partially right. Gradually, she practiced replacing black-and-white thinking with more nuanced views, focusing on progress and partial successes rather than perfection.

Another common distortion is catastrophizing, where individuals envision the worst possible outcome, regardless of the actual likelihood. Ben's experience with catastrophizing sheds light on how this pattern can be altered. He constantly worried about minor symptoms, fearing they indicated severe illness. This led him to avoid social interactions, convinced he would embarrass himself or worse, fall sick in public. His turning point came when he began therapy and was introduced to realistic assessments of his fears.

Ben embarked on the process by examining the actual probability of his catastrophic thoughts materializing. He logged his fears and worked on evaluating their realism. His therapist guided him through controlled exposure to feared situations, helping him realize that catastrophe rarely struck. Ben also learned mindfulness and relaxation techniques to manage his anxiety whenever catastrophic thoughts surfaced.

Demonstrating the process of confronting exaggerated fears involves breaking down these fears into manageable parts. Ben started small, attending brief social events and gradually increasing his participation. With each successful encounter, he recorded his experiences, reinforcing positive outcomes over imagined disasters. Developing resilience came from this repeated practice, proving to him that his fears were often unfounded. Over time, Ben built confidence and reduced his tendency to catastrophize.

Understanding and applying techniques to challenge cognitive distortions can significantly improve mental well-being.

Throughout this chapter, we have explored several cognitive distortions and how they shape our thoughts and emotions. From all-or-nothing thinking to catastrophizing, personalization, and filtering, each of these patterns can significantly impact our mental well-being if left unchecked.

We began by understanding that recognizing these distortions is the first step toward overcoming them. By identifying when we fall into black-and-white thinking, we can find a middle ground that allows for a more balanced perspective. This shift helps alleviate feelings of inadequacy and stress by giving us a more nuanced view of situations.

Challenging these thoughts involves asking ourselves questions that promote nuance and realism. For instance, when faced with all-or-nothing thinking, we should consider what went well and where there's room for improvement. This approach reduces the stress associated with rigid thinking and helps us see the broader picture.

Catastrophizing was another key topic. We learned that predicting the worst possible outcome often leads to excessive anxiety and fear. By evaluating the likelihood of these catastrophic scenarios and considering best-case and most likely outcomes, we can reduce unnecessary worry. This method of confronting exaggerated fears helps us maintain a more balanced outlook on life.

Personalization, or taking responsibility for events beyond our control, also came under scrutiny. Understanding that not everything revolves around us can be liberating. Acknowledging that other people have their own lives, choices, and reasons for their actions allows us to let go of unnecessary guilt or blame, improving our self-esteem.

Filtering, the tendency to focus solely on negative details while ignoring positive aspects, was the last distortion we discussed. Practicing gratitude and making a conscious effort to recognize and appreciate positive elements in our lives can shift our focus from what's missing to what's abundant.

Moving forward, it's vital to apply these insights actively. Mindfulness practice can help us stay present and observe our thoughts without judgment, providing clarity on how our thought patterns affect our emotions and behaviors. Emotional awareness, by focusing on physical sensations and reactions, deepens our understanding of how feelings influence our thoughts.

Journaling offers an effective way to externalize and analyze our thoughts, revealing patterns that need addressing. Keeping a thought journal helps us track our progress and reinforces healthy thought patterns over time.

Inconsistent reality testing, seeking feedback from others, and engaging in behaviors that contradict our negative thoughts further aid us in recalibrating our perceptions. The support of friends, family, and professionals can provide valuable perspectives and guidance, helping us challenge and reframe distorted views.

By understanding and challenging cognitive distortions, we pave the way for better mental health and a more positive mindset. This journey doesn't end here; it's an ongoing process of self-awareness and growth. As you move forward, remember that change takes time and patience. With consistent effort, you can transform your thought patterns and cultivate a healthier, happier mind.

While cognitive distortions are common, breaking free from these harmful patterns can lead to profound personal development. Embrace these techniques, seek support when needed, and continue exploring ways to nurture your mental well-being. The path to a more balanced and positive mindset is within your reach, and every step you take brings you closer to achieving it.

Chapter 4

The Power of Cognitive Behavioral Therapy (CBT)

Understanding the power of Cognitive Behavioral Therapy (CBT) involves delving into its ability to change negative thought patterns and improve mental health. Originating from the integration of behaviorism and cognitive psychology, CBT has developed into an evidence-based therapy widely recognized for its effectiveness across various mental health conditions. By examining the basic concepts and techniques used in CBT, we can gain insight into why it remains a cornerstone in the treatment of anxiety, depression, and more.

In this chapter, we will explore the history and principles that form the foundation of CBT. We'll take a journey through its origins, tracing back to the mid-20th century when psychologists began merging behavioral theories with cognitive processes. The chapter also sheds light on key figures like Aaron Beck and Albert Ellis, whose pioneering work significantly shaped CBT. Additionally, we'll investigate the core principles, such as cognitive restructuring and the importance of the therapist-client relationship, and discuss how these elements contribute to changing negative thought patterns. This comprehensive overview helps us appreciate the scientific foundation and practical applications that make CBT a powerful tool for improving mental well-being.

History and principles of CBT

Cognitive Behavioral Therapy (CBT) has evolved into one of the most effective treatments for tackling negative thought patterns and improving mental health. To understand its impact, it is essential to explore its origins and core tenets.

The origins of CBT trace back to behaviorism and cognitive psychology. Initially, behaviorism focused on observable behaviors and how they are learned from the environment. This approach was pivotal in understanding human behavior but often neglected internal thoughts and feelings. Cognitive psychology, on the other hand, delved into the intricacies of mental processes like thinking, memory, and problem-solving. In the mid-20th century, psychologists started combining these two approaches, leading to the development of CBT. It aimed to address both the behavioral aspects and the underlying cognitive processes that contribute to psychological issues. Aaron Beck, a key figure in this integration, noticed that patients with depression exhibited consistent patterns of distorted thinking. His work laid the groundwork for

CBT by integrating cognitive theories with behavioral techniques.

Core principles of CBT include cognitive restructuring, which involves identifying and challenging irrational beliefs. At its heart, CBT posits that our thoughts influence our emotions and behaviors. This principle is encapsulated in the concept of automatic thoughts—spontaneous, often subconscious, interpretations of events that can shape our emotional responses. For instance, if someone interprets a brief interaction as a sign of rejection, this negative thought can lead to feelings of sadness or worthlessness. By recognizing and altering these thoughts, individuals can change their emotional and behavioral responses. Another principle is the collaborative nature of the therapist-client relationship. In CBT, therapists work closely with clients to set realistic goals and develop strategies for change. This partnership ensures that therapy is tailored to the individual's specific needs and promotes active participation in the therapeutic process.

The evidence-based approach in CBT emphasizes the importance of empirical research in developing and validating its techniques. Numerous studies have demonstrated the efficacy of CBT in treating a wide range of mental health conditions, from depression and anxiety to post-traumatic stress disorder (PTSD) and obsessive-compulsive disorder (OCD). For example, randomized controlled trials have shown that CBT can be as effective as medication for some individuals with moderate to severe depression. These findings underscore the scientific foundation of CBT, which relies on measurable outcomes and continuous refinement based on research. This rigorous approach not only supports the effectiveness of CBT but also helps in customizing treatment protocols to suit different disorders and populations.

Key figures in the development of CBT principles include Aaron Beck and Albert Ellis. Beck, often regarded as the father of CBT, introduced the concept of cognitive distortions and developed structured therapy sessions aimed at correcting faulty thinking patterns. His contributions provided a systematic framework for understanding and addressing cognitive errors associated with various mental health conditions. Albert Ellis, another pioneering figure, developed Rational Emotive Behavior Therapy (REBT), which shares many similarities with CBT. Ellis emphasized the role of irrational beliefs in emotional distress and advocated for the use of logical analysis to challenge and change these beliefs. Both Beck and Ellis contributed significantly to the theoretical and practical foundations of CBT, shaping it into a widely accepted and effective therapeutic approach.

Understanding the evolution of CBT from behaviorism and cognitive psychology highlights its comprehensive approach to mental health. By integrating insights from both disciplines, CBT addresses the multifaceted nature of psychological issues, focusing on observable behaviors and underlying cognitive processes. This dual focus allows for a more holistic understanding of how thoughts and behaviors interplay in contributing to emotional distress.

Delving into the core principles of CBT, such as cognitive restructuring, reveals how powerful changing thought patterns can be. Cognitive restructuring empowers individuals to identify and alter negative thoughts that perpetuate emotional suffering. By transforming these thoughts, individuals can experience significant improvements in their emotional well-being and overall quality of life. This process not only alleviates symptoms but also provides individuals with tools to manage future challenges effectively.

Emphasizing the empirical basis of CBT underscores its credibility and reliability as a therapeutic approach. The robust body of research supporting CBT demonstrates its effectiveness across various populations and conditions. This evidence-based foundation ensures that CBT practices are continually refined and updated based on the latest scientific findings, enhancing their relevance and applicability in real-world settings.

Highlighting key figures like Aaron Beck and Albert Ellis provides insight into the foundational theories and innovations that shaped CBT. Their groundbreaking work laid the theoretical and practical groundwork for CBT, establishing it as a structured, goal-oriented, and empirically validated form of therapy. By examining their contributions, we gain a deeper appreciation for the development and evolution of CBT principles.

How CBT works

Cognitive Behavioral Therapy (CBT) operates through a variety of mechanisms to help individuals change negative thought patterns. One primary method is cognitive restructuring, which involves identifying and challenging irrational beliefs. The process begins with recognizing automatic thoughts that often occur as immediate reactions to situations. These thoughts may be distorted or overly negative, leading to heightened anxiety or depression.

Once identified, these irrational beliefs are carefully examined for their validity. The therapist and individual work together to question the evidence supporting these beliefs and consider alternative, more realistic perspectives. This technique helps in reducing the intensity of negative emotions associated with the irrational thoughts.

An essential aspect of cognitive restructuring is replacing harmful thoughts with positive and balanced ones. As individuals practice this skill, they become more adept at shifting their mental focus, which can lead to long-term changes in their overall thought patterns and emotional responses. By consistently applying cognitive restructuring techniques, individuals gradually develop healthier ways of thinking.

Behavioral activation is another critical component of CBT that addresses negative thought patterns through action. It emphasizes the connection between behavior and mood, and how changes in activity levels can influence thoughts and feelings. Behavioral experiments are designed to test the accuracy of beliefs and challenge avoidance behaviors.

Exposure techniques are also frequently employed in behavioral activation. These involve gradually facing feared situations in a controlled manner, which helps in reducing anxiety over time. For instance, someone with social anxiety might start by engaging in small social interactions and then progressively face more challenging scenarios.

The ultimate goal of behavioral activation is to increase engagement in positive activities, which can improve mood and reinforce positive thinking. By systematically engaging in rewarding activities, individuals can break the cycle of negativity and build more constructive habits.

Homework assignments in CBT play a vital role in reinforcing the skills learned during therapy sessions. These tasks are designed to provide practice opportunities outside the therapeutic setting, ensuring that the techniques become ingrained in everyday life. Common homework assignments might include keeping thought records, practicing relaxation exercises, or completing specific behavioral experiments.

Consistent practice of these assignments can significantly impact the effectiveness of CBT. As individuals repeatedly apply the strategies they've learned, they become more proficient in managing their thoughts and behaviors. This consistent effort is crucial in creating lasting change.

Moreover, homework assignments help bridge the gap between therapy sessions, maintaining momentum and progress. They encourage individuals to take an active role in their treatment, fostering a sense of empowerment and self-efficacy. By diligently working on these tasks, individuals can accelerate their progress and achieve better outcomes.

Understanding cognitive distortions is fundamental in addressing negative thought patterns within CBT. Cognitive distortions are habitual errors in thinking that reinforce negative beliefs and emotions. They include common patterns such as overgeneralization, catastrophizing, and black-and-white thinking.

Recognizing these distortions is the first step towards changing them. By becoming aware of these faulty thinking patterns, individuals can begin to question and challenge them. This awareness allows for more rational and balanced thinking, reducing the influence of cognitive distortions on one's emotional state.

Addressing cognitive distortions also involves developing coping strategies to manage stress and anxiety more effectively. Techniques like mindfulness and self-compassion can be integrated into CBT to help individuals stay present and avoid being consumed by negative thoughts. These strategies foster resilience and promote a more positive outlook on life.

Examples of successful CBT applications

Cognitive Behavioral Therapy (CBT) has proven to be a game-changer in treating anxiety disorders. Take the case of Anna, a 30-year-old teacher struggling with generalized anxiety disorder. She experienced constant worry about her job performance and health, making it difficult for her to function daily. Through CBT, Anna learned to identify her negative thought patterns, such as catastrophizing every minor mistake at work. With the help of her therapist, she practiced challenging these thoughts and replaced them with more balanced perspectives. Over time, Anna noticed a significant reduction in her anxiety levels, allowing her to engage more fully in her teaching duties and social activities.

Another illustrative scenario involves Mark, who suffered from social anxiety disorder. Mark dreaded social interactions, fearing judgment and rejection by others. His CBT sessions included exposure exercises where he gradually faced situations he avoided, like speaking up in meetings or attending social gatherings. Accompanied by cognitive restructuring techniques, Mark began to see these social events as less threatening. He recorded his thoughts and outcomes in a journal, which helped reinforce the positive experiences and debunked his irrational fears. After several months, Mark found himself more comfortable engaging with colleagues and friends, experiencing fewer episodes of debilitating anxiety.

CBT's effectiveness extends to panic disorder as well, illustrated by the story of Lisa. Lisa had frequent panic attacks that made her fear leaving her home. Her therapist employed interoceptive exposure, where Lisa intentionally induced physical sensations similar to those of a panic attack, such as rapid breathing. By doing this in a controlled environment, Lisa learned that these sensations were not dangerous. Coupled with cognitive restructuring to address her fear of having a heart attack, Lisa's panic symptoms decreased dramatically. She regained her confidence to step out of her home and participate in activities she once enjoyed.

Depressive symptoms also show marked improvement through CBT interventions. Consider John, who battled persistent feelings of hopelessness and lack of interest in daily activities. John's therapist guided him through identifying automatic negative thoughts, such as "I am worthless" and "Things will never get better." By challenging these thoughts and finding evidence against them, John slowly began to adopt a more optimistic outlook. Behavioral activation was another crucial component of his therapy, as John was encouraged to engage in activities he previously enjoyed, even if he didn't feel like it initially. This combination of strategies led to a noticeable uplift in John's mood and energy levels over time.

In another example, Sarah suffered from postpartum depression, overwhelmed by feelings of inadequacy as a new mother. Through CBT, Sarah worked on changing her self-critical thoughts, like "I'm a terrible mother," into more compassionate ones. Her therapist also introduced mindfulness techniques to help Sarah stay grounded and reduce rumination. Gradually, Sarah experienced an increase in her self-esteem and felt more capable in her parenting role. The structured nature of CBT provided Sarah with practical tools to manage her depressive symptoms effectively.

The case of Kevin illustrates CBT's impact on severe depression linked to job loss. Kevin felt paralyzed by guilt and failure after being laid off. His therapist focused on reinterpreting his thoughts around this event, helping him understand that losing his job did not define his worth. Kevin was also taught problem-solving skills, enabling him to take small, actionable steps towards finding new employment. These steps included updating his resume, networking, and applying for jobs. As a result, Kevin's motivation returned, and his depressive symptoms lessened, leading him to successfully secure new employment.

CBT is highly effective in treating phobias, as seen in Emily's case, who had a debilitating fear of flying. Emily's treatment involved gradual exposure to flying-related stimuli, starting with looking at pictures of airplanes and eventually booking a short flight. Throughout this process, her therapist guided her in using relaxation techniques and cognitive restructuring to challenge her catastrophic thoughts, like the plane crashing. By facing her fear in manageable steps, Emily overcame her phobia and was able to fly comfortably for the first time in years.

Similarly, Jason's intense fear of spiders was addressed through CBT. His therapist employed systematic desensitization, where Jason was exposed to spiders in a controlled manner, starting with images and moving to real-life encounters. By combining this with cognitive restructuring, Jason learned to reinterpret his exaggerated fears about spiders harming him. Over time, his anxiety reduced significantly, enabling him to handle situations involving spiders without panic.

Megan's experience with a severe driving phobia shows how CBT can facilitate long-term change. Megan avoided driving for years due to a previous accident. Her CBT sessions included both in vivo exposure, where she started with sitting in a parked car, and imaginal exposure, revisiting the accident in her mind. Guided by her therapist, Megan worked through her trauma and irrational fears. This methodical approach helped Megan regain her confidence in driving, ultimately restoring her independence.

Obsessive-Compulsive Disorder (OCD) also responds well to CBT techniques like exposure and response prevention (EX/RP). For instance, David had obsessive thoughts about contaminating his hands, leading to excessive washing. In EX/RP therapy, David was exposed to contaminants, such as touching doorknobs, without performing the compulsive handwashing. This practice allowed him to experience and tolerate the anxiety until it naturally subsided, breaking the cycle of obsession and compulsion.

Emma's OCD manifested in checking behaviors, such as repeatedly ensuring the stove was turned off. Her therapist used imaginal exposure, where Emma imagined the consequences of not checking the stove, paired with response prevention, refraining from checking. Over time, this reduced her compulsions and associated anxiety. Emma learned to trust her initial actions, significantly improving her daily functioning.

Lastly, Michael's intrusive thoughts about harming others were addressed through CBT. His treatment involved exposing him to feared situations, like holding a knife in a safe setting, while preventing any safety behaviors that mitigated his anxiety. Cognitive restructuring was used to challenge his beliefs about losing control. This comprehensive approach led to a substantial decrease in Michael's distressing thoughts and compulsions, illustrating the profound impact of CBT.

CBT techniques for everyday use

Cognitive Behavioral Therapy (CBT) offers various practical strategies to help individuals combat negative thoughts. One of the primary tools used in CBT is thought records. Thought records are designed to track and challenge negative thoughts, providing a structured format for identifying unhelpful thinking patterns. By writing down situations that trigger negative emotions, individuals can examine their initial thoughts and evaluate the evidence supporting or refuting these thoughts. This method encourages a more balanced perspective, transforming automatic negative thoughts into more rational and constructive ones.

To effectively use thought records, it is important to follow a step-by-step approach. Start by identifying a situation that has triggered a strong emotional response. Next, record the automatic thoughts that arose during this event. These thoughts often contain cognitive distortions, such as overgeneralization or catastrophic thinking. Then, assess the emotional intensity and identify corresponding physical sensations. Finally, examine the evidence for and against these automatic thoughts, and generate alternative, more balanced thoughts. Doing this consistently helps create new, healthier thought patterns.

Offering readers templates and examples can be very helpful in practicing thought records. For instance, a template might include columns for recording the situation, automatic thoughts, emotional responses, evidence for and against the thoughts, and alternative thoughts. Real-life examples demonstrating how others have successfully used thought records can provide guidance and motivation. By incorporating thought records into daily routines, individuals can gradually reframe their thinking and reduce the impact of negative thoughts on their lives.

Another effective CBT strategy is conducting behavioral experiments. Behavioral experiments allow individuals to test the validity of their negative beliefs through real-world actions. These experiments involve predicting outcomes based on negative beliefs, engaging in specific behaviors, and then observing the actual outcomes. This process helps challenge and often disprove inaccurate or exaggerated thoughts, fostering a more realistic understanding of situations.

Designing and carrying out personal experiments requires careful planning. First, identify a negative belief you want to test. Next, predict what will happen if you act contrary to this belief. For example, if you believe that speaking up at a meeting will result in ridicule, your experiment might involve sharing an idea during the next meeting. Record your predictions and feelings before and after the action to compare expectations with reality. This reflective practice not only provides evidence against negative thoughts but also builds confidence in facing challenging situations.

Gathering evidence to support or refute negative thoughts is crucial in behavioral experiments. It's important to remain objective and open-minded when evaluating outcomes. If the results of an experiment don't align with your expectations, analyze why that may be and whether your initial belief might be flawed. Over time, accumulating positive experiences from behavioral experiments can weaken the hold of negative thoughts and promote a healthier mindset.

Integrating mindfulness practices with CBT techniques further enhances self-awareness and cognitive flexibility. Mindfulness involves focusing on the present moment with an attitude of non-judgmental acceptance. By cultivating mindfulness, individuals can become more aware of their thoughts and feelings without immediately reacting to them. This awareness creates space to choose more adaptive responses, reducing the power of automatic negative thoughts.

Mindfulness can enhance the effectiveness of CBT by increasing self-awareness. When individuals are mindful, they are better able to observe their thoughts and emotions as they arise. This heightened awareness makes it easier to identify cognitive distortions and apply CBT techniques like thought records or behavioral experiments. Moreover, mindfulness practice can improve emotional regulation, helping individuals stay calm and grounded even in stressful situations.

Guiding readers on incorporating mindfulness into their CBT toolkit can foster sustained well-being. Simple mindfulness exercises, such as focused breathing or body scans, can be integrated into daily routines. Encouraging readers to set aside a few minutes each day for mindfulness practice can lead to significant benefits over time. As mindfulness becomes a habit, it reinforces the cognitive restructuring and behavioral changes promoted by CBT, creating a holistic approach to managing negative thoughts.

Practice strategies are essential for reinforcing CBT techniques outside therapy sessions. Consistency and repetition are key to making lasting changes in thought patterns. Encouraging readers to set specific goals for practicing CBT strategies can help integrate these techniques into their daily lives. For example, setting a goal to complete a thought record twice a week can make the practice more manageable and routine.

Developing a support system can also enhance the practice of CBT techniques. Sharing goals and progress with friends, family, or a therapist can provide accountability and encouragement. Joining a support group or online community focused on CBT can offer additional resources and insights. Regularly discussing challenges and successes with others can help maintain motivation and reinforce positive changes.

Finally, emphasizing the importance of self-compassion in practicing CBT techniques can prevent burnout and frustration. Change takes time, and setbacks are a natural part of the process. Encouraging readers to approach themselves with kindness and patience can make the journey more sustainable. Practicing self-compassion involves treating oneself with the same understanding and care one would offer to a friend, recognizing that everyone struggles and that imperfections do not define worth.

Readers will gain a foundational understanding of CBT's history, principles, and evidence-based approach to tackling negative thought patterns.

We have explored the roots and principles of Cognitive Behavioral Therapy (CBT), understanding how it has evolved from behaviorism and cognitive psychology. By merging these two schools of thought, CBT offers a comprehensive approach to tackling negative thought patterns and improving mental health. The pioneering work of Aaron Beck and Albert Ellis has allowed us to better grasp the importance of restructuring our thoughts to positively influence our emotions and behaviors.

One of the key takeaways from our dive into CBT is the transformative potential of cognitive restructuring. This practice teaches us to identify irrational beliefs and replace them with more balanced perspectives. By doing so, we can significantly alter our emotional and behavioral responses, leading to improved mental well-being. The concept of automatic thoughts, often subconscious and immediate reactions, underscores how deeply ingrained our thought patterns can be and how crucial it is to address them.

Another vital aspect of CBT is its empirical foundation. Countless studies back the effectiveness of CBT across various mental health conditions such as depression, anxiety, PTSD, and OCD. This rigorous scientific support not only reinforces the validity of CBT but also helps ensure that its techniques are continuously refined for better outcomes. The evidence-based nature of CBT means that practices are not stagnant; they evolve with research, tailoring them to suit diverse needs and disorders.

While we have discussed the theoretical aspects of CBT, it is essential to recognize its practical applications through real-world examples and success stories. Understanding the process of identifying and challenging cognitive distortions highlights the importance of self-awareness in managing stress and anxiety. Techniques like mindfulness and self-compassion further enrich CBT by promoting resilience and a positive outlook on life.

For those struggling with negative thought patterns, the journey does not end here. It is important to remain curious and open-minded about incorporating CBT techniques into everyday life. Engaging in thought records, conducting behavioral experiments, and practicing mindfulness are all actionable steps toward achieving a healthier mindset. Setting realistic goals and maintaining consistency in applying these techniques can lead to lasting change.

As we conclude this chapter, consider how the principles of CBT could impact your daily life. Reflect on any automatic thoughts or cognitive distortions you might have and think about how restructuring these thoughts could improve your emotional well-being. Remember that therapy is a collaborative effort between the therapist and the client, ensuring personalized approaches tailored to your unique experiences.

Ultimately, CBT provides tools for lifelong mental health improvement. By understanding its principles and actively practicing its techniques, you can cultivate a positive mindset and build resilience against future challenges. As you continue reading, keep these concepts in mind and explore how they might integrate into your personal development journey.

Chapter 5

Developing Emotional Resilience

Developing emotional resilience is a key skill in navigating the ups and downs of life. It's about having the ability to bounce back from stress, adversity, and challenging situations without feeling overwhelmed. This chapter delves into the practical tools and techniques that can help cultivate this essential quality. By focusing on methods derived from mindfulness practices and Cognitive Behavioral Therapy (CBT), we explore ways to build that mental muscle which is crucial for maintaining mental well-being.

In this chapter, you will learn how cognitive restructuring, a core CBT technique, can help shift negative thought patterns to more positive and balanced ones. We'll also cover various mindfulness exercises, such as deep breathing and body scans, which aid in staying present and reducing stress. Additionally, the importance of self-compassion and gratitude journaling will be highlighted as means to nurture inner strength and positivity. Through these approaches, you'll find effective strategies to become more resilient, handle life's challenges with grace, and improve your overall mental health.

What is emotional resilience?

Emotional resilience refers to the ability to adapt and recover from stress, adversity, and challenging situations. It's like a mental muscle that helps you bounce back from difficult experiences and maintain a sense of well-being. This concept is crucial in managing everyday stresses and significant life events, as it allows individuals to navigate through tough times without being overwhelmed.

Understanding emotional resilience begins with recognizing its components. It involves a combination of mental toughness, optimism, and the capacity to manage emotions effectively. Emotional resilience doesn't mean avoiding or suppressing difficult feelings; rather, it's about experiencing and processing these emotions constructively. This quality is essential for maintaining mental health because it helps prevent the buildup of stress, which can lead to anxiety and depression if left unchecked.

The significance of emotional resilience lies in its widespread impact on various aspects of life. When individuals are resilient, they are better equipped to handle workplace pressures, relational conflicts, and personal challenges. This ability to manage stress not only fosters psychological well-being but also contributes to physical health by reducing the risk of stress-related illnesses. Thus, cultivating emotional resilience is vital for anyone looking to improve their overall quality of life.

Resilient individuals often share several key characteristics that enable them to handle difficulties effectively. One such trait is self-awareness; they have a deep understanding of their strengths and weaknesses, which allows them to approach problems with a clear perspective. This self-awareness also helps them regulate their emotions and reactions, preventing impulsive decisions during stressful times.

Another important characteristic is optimism. Resilient people tend to maintain a positive outlook even when faced with setbacks. They see challenges as opportunities for growth rather than insurmountable obstacles. This optimistic attitude fuels their perseverance, helping them stay motivated to overcome difficulties. Additionally, they possess strong problem-solving skills, enabling them to identify potential solutions and take proactive steps to address issues.

Social support is also a critical component of resilience. Resilient individuals actively seek and maintain supportive relationships. These connections provide emotional and practical assistance, creating a safety net that reinforces their ability to cope with adversity. Having a strong support system encourages open communication, shared experiences, and mutual encouragement, all of which are invaluable when navigating life's ups and downs.

The impact of emotional resilience on well-being is profound. For starters, resilient people experience lower levels of stress and anxiety. By effectively managing their emotions and responses to stressors, they avoid the negative spiral of chronic stress, which can severely impact both mental and physical health. Reduced stress levels contribute to better sleep, improved focus, and enhanced cognitive function, all of which are essential for daily performance and long-term success.

Moreover, emotional resilience enhances overall life satisfaction. When individuals can face challenges head-on and bounce back from setbacks, they feel more in control of their lives. This sense of control and competence boosts self-esteem and confidence, leading to greater happiness and fulfillment. Resilient individuals are more likely to engage in activities they enjoy and pursue meaningful goals, further increasing their sense of purpose and joy.

Another benefit is the promotion of healthier relationships. Emotional resilience leads to better emotional regulation and communication skills, which are crucial for building and maintaining strong interpersonal connections. Resilient people are more capable of resolving conflicts, expressing empathy, and providing support to others. These positive interactions foster deeper, more satisfying relationships that contribute to overall well-being.

Skills to develop resilience

One of the most powerful tools in Cognitive Behavioral Therapy (CBT) for enhancing emotional resilience is cognitive restructuring. This technique involves identifying and challenging negative thought patterns, which can often contribute to feelings of anxiety, stress, and low self-esteem. When we repeatedly think negatively, these thoughts can become automatic and deeply ingrained, making it difficult to cope with life's challenges. By learning to recognize these patterns, we can begin to question and reframe them, leading to more balanced and positive thinking.

To get started with cognitive restructuring, it's helpful to keep a thought diary. In this diary, you can jot down any distressing thoughts as they arise, note the situation in which they occurred, and rate the intensity of the emotion associated with the thought. Once you've identified a negative thought, challenge its validity. Ask yourself questions like, "Is there evidence supporting this thought?" or "Am I jumping to conclusions?" By doing so, you might find that many of your negative thoughts are exaggerated or inaccurate. Over time, practicing this exercise can help shift your mindset and bolster your emotional resilience.

Another key aspect of cognitive restructuring is replacing negative thoughts with more constructive ones. For example, if you catch yourself thinking, "I'll never be good enough," try to counter this with a more realistic and positive thought, such as, "I have strengths and areas where I can improve." This process helps to create new neural pathways in the brain, making it easier to adopt a more optimistic outlook. As you continue to practice cognitive restructuring, you'll likely find that you're better equipped to handle setbacks and navigate life's ups and downs with greater emotional strength.

In addition to cognitive restructuring, mindfulness practices play a vital role in building emotional resilience. Mindfulness involves paying attention to the present moment without judgment, which can help reduce stress and enhance overall mental well-being. One simple yet effective mindfulness exercise is deep breathing. Sit comfortably, close your eyes, and take slow, deep breaths, focusing on the sensation of the air entering and leaving your body. This practice can help calm your mind and bring you back to the present, making it easier to manage stress.

Another valuable mindfulness technique is the body scan. This involves mentally scanning your body from head to toe, noticing any sensations or areas of tension without trying to change anything. To practice a body scan, find a quiet space, lie down, and begin by focusing on your toes. Gradually work your way up through your legs, torso, arms, and head, taking time to observe each part of your body. This exercise can increase your awareness of physical sensations and promote relaxation, contributing to greater emotional resilience.

Mindfulness meditation is also highly beneficial. Set aside a few minutes each day to sit quietly and focus on your breath, allowing thoughts to come and go without getting caught up in them. If your mind wanders, gently bring your attention back to your breath. This practice can help you develop a sense of inner calm and centeredness, which is invaluable when facing life's stresses. By incorporating mindfulness into your daily routine, you'll cultivate a heightened awareness and presence, enabling you to respond to challenges with greater clarity and composure.

Self-compassion techniques are equally important for fostering emotional resilience. Treating yourself with kindness and understanding, especially during difficult times, can have a profound impact on your ability to bounce back from adversity. One effective method for cultivating self-compassion is self-kindness. Instead of being overly critical of yourself when things go wrong, try speaking to yourself in a supportive and comforting manner, much like you would with a close friend. This gentler approach can alleviate feelings of inadequacy and foster a more resilient mindset.

Another approach to self-compassion is recognizing our shared humanity. Understand that everyone experiences hardship and makes mistakes; it's a natural part of being human. By acknowledging that struggle is a common experience, you can feel less isolated in your difficulties and more connected to others. This perspective can lessen the burden of self-criticism and boost your ability to handle challenges with grace and resilience.

Daily practices for strengthening resilience

One of the most effective strategies for fostering emotional resilience is the practice of gratitude journaling. Gratitude journaling involves regularly writing down things you are thankful for. This simple yet powerful exercise helps shift focus from negative thoughts, which often dominate our minds, to positive aspects of life. By recognizing and acknowledging what we appreciate, we start to cultivate a mindset geared towards positivity and contentment.

To begin gratitude journaling, set aside a few minutes each day to reflect on your experiences. Consider both big and small moments that brought you joy, comfort, or a sense of accomplishment. Write them down in a dedicated journal. You might feel grateful for a supportive friend, a warm meal, or even a moment of peace in an otherwise hectic day. The key is consistency; making this a daily habit can significantly alter your perspective over time.

The benefits of gratitude journaling are backed by research. Studies show that people who practice gratitude regularly experience lower levels of stress and depression. Their overall well-being improves, and they exhibit greater resilience when faced with challenges. By focusing on positive experiences, gratitude journaling trains the brain to seek out and recognize good in various situations, thus building emotional resilience.

Breathing exercises are another valuable tool for stress relief and emotional regulation. When we are stressed, our breathing often becomes shallow and rapid, signaling to our body that something is wrong. By consciously controlling our breath, we can calm our nervous system and reduce stress. There are several breathing techniques that can be easily incorporated into daily routines to enhance emotional resilience.

One popular method is diaphragmatic breathing, also known as belly breathing. Sit or lie down comfortably and place one hand on your chest and the other on your abdomen. Take a slow, deep breath through your nose, allowing your diaphragm (not your chest) to inflate with air. Exhale slowly through your mouth. Repeat this process for a few minutes, focusing on the rise and fall of your abdomen. This technique helps to engage the parasympathetic nervous system, promoting relaxation and reducing anxiety.

Another effective technique is the 4-7-8 breathing method. Inhale quietly through your nose for a count of four, hold your breath for a count of seven, and then exhale completely through your mouth for a count of eight. This pattern promotes deep relaxation and can be particularly useful during moments of acute stress or before sleep. Regular practice can help create a more balanced emotional state, thereby enhancing your ability to stay resilient in difficult situations.

Positive affirmations are powerful statements that individuals can repeat to themselves to combat negative thoughts and reinforce a positive mindset. They work by challenging and replacing harmful beliefs or self-doubt with empowering truths. Incorporating positive affirmations into your daily routine can play a significant role in building emotional resilience.

To use positive affirmations effectively, first identify areas where you feel challenged or insecure. Craft affirmations that directly counter these feelings. For instance, if you struggle with self-esteem, an affirmation might be, "I am worthy and capable of achieving my goals." Repeat your affirmations daily, ideally in front of a mirror, to reinforce their message. Consistency is crucial, as repeated exposure helps rewire your thinking patterns.

It's important to choose affirmations that resonate deeply with you. Personalize them to reflect your unique aspirations and strengths. This personalization makes the affirmations more impactful and believable. Over time, these affirmations can help shift your inner dialogue from negative and self-critical to positive and supportive, aiding in emotional resilience.

Real-life applications of resilience techniques

One of the most common environments where emotional resilience is tested is the workplace. Many individuals face pressures such as tight deadlines, heavy workloads, and even interpersonal conflicts with colleagues or supervisors. By employing resilience techniques, it becomes possible to navigate these challenges more effectively. One essential method is mindfulness, which helps in staying present and focused, thereby reducing overall stress. For instance, taking a few moments throughout the day for deep breathing exercises can significantly lower anxiety levels, allowing one to approach tasks with a calm and clear mind.

Another key technique is Cognitive Behavioral Therapy (CBT), specifically the practice of cognitive restructuring. This involves identifying and challenging negative thought patterns that can exacerbate stress. For example, instead of thinking "I will never finish this project on time," one can reframe the thought to "I have faced tough deadlines before and managed them well." Such reframing not only reduces the sense of panic but also boosts self-confidence and ability to handle pressure. Real-life applications of these techniques prove invaluable, whether preparing for an important presentation or managing daily tasks.

Implementing these strategies in the workplace isn't just about personal relief; it also contributes to a more positive work environment. When employees manage their stress effectively, they are less likely to experience burnout and more likely to engage productively. Moreover, resilience equips individuals to handle unexpected changes or failures gracefully, turning potential setbacks into opportunities for growth and learning. Over time, practicing these techniques makes them second nature, building a more resilient mindset that benefits both personal and professional life.

In relationships, emotional resilience plays a crucial role in managing conflicts and maintaining healthy dynamics. Conflicts are inevitable in any close relationship, but how we respond to them can make all the difference. Mindfulness practices, such as active listening and staying present during conversations, can help in understanding the other person's perspective without jumping to conclusions or reacting emotionally. This mindful approach fosters empathy and opens the door to constructive dialogue rather than escalating tensions.

Another effective technique is utilizing CBT tools like reframing and problem-solving. For example, if a partner's remark feels hurtful, instead of immediately reacting defensively, one could take a step back and consider alternative interpretations of the comment. Perhaps the partner is stressed about something unrelated, and the perceived slight was not intentional.

Approaching conflicts with this mindset allows individuals to address issues more calmly and find mutually beneficial solutions. Thus, emotional resilience can transform potentially damaging confrontations into opportunities for deeper connection and understanding.

Practicing self-compassion is equally vital when dealing with relationship struggles. Often, individuals are hard on themselves, blaming themselves entirely for conflicts. Adopting a kinder, more forgiving attitude towards oneself helps in managing emotions better and prevents the downward spiral of negative self-talk. By being gentle with oneself and recognizing that everyone makes mistakes, it becomes easier to navigate relationship challenges without additional emotional burden. Ultimately, fostering emotional resilience in relationships enhances overall satisfaction and stability, promoting a healthier and more fulfilling bond.

During personal crises, emotional resilience techniques become a lifeline, providing much-needed support and stability. Crises such as losing a loved one, facing serious health issues, or experiencing significant life changes can be overwhelming. Mindfulness practices can be profoundly grounding in such situations. Engaging in mindful meditation or simply focusing on the breath can offer moments of peace amidst chaos, helping individuals to stay centered and manage their emotional responses more effectively.

Cognitive Behavioral Therapy offers essential tools for coping during personal crises as well. Techniques like thought records can be particularly helpful. Keeping a journal to track thoughts and feelings allows individuals to process their experiences and identify negative thought patterns. By examining these thoughts critically and reframing them, one can prevent spiraling into despair. For instance, changing a thought from "I'll never get through this" to "This is extremely difficult, but I have the strength to cope" can be incredibly empowering, fostering a sense of control and hope.

Readers will gain an understanding of emotional resilience and its significance in fostering mental strength and well-being.

We've explored how mindfulness and Cognitive Behavioral Therapy (CBT) can help build emotional resilience. Through understanding its components like mental toughness, optimism, and effective emotion management, we've seen why emotional resilience is essential for maintaining mental well-being. This chapter has also shown that resilient individuals tend to have self-awareness, optimism, strong problem-solving skills, and supportive relationships.

By utilizing tools such as cognitive restructuring, one can identify and challenge negative thought patterns, making it easier to handle stress and setbacks. Techniques like keeping a thought diary and practicing constructive thinking can shift our mindset towards positivity. Likewise, mindfulness practices such as deep breathing, body scans, and meditation contribute to a calmer and more present mental state, aiding in stress reduction and emotional regulation. Self-compassion adds another layer, helping us treat ourselves with kindness during hard times.

Daily practices like gratitude journaling, diaphragmatic breathing, and positive affirmations can further strengthen emotional resilience. These habits train our brains to focus on the positive and manage stress effectively, which is crucial for overall well-being. Real-life applications in the workplace and personal relationships highlight how these techniques can be employed to handle pressure, resolve conflicts, and maintain healthy dynamics. Whether it's managing deadlines, dealing with interpersonal issues, or facing personal crises, these skills provide a toolkit for navigating life's challenges.

It's important to remember that building emotional resilience is not about avoiding or suppressing difficult feelings. Rather, it's about experiencing and processing emotions constructively. Some readers may find it challenging to adopt these new habits, particularly if they are accustomed to negative thought patterns. However, the potential consequences of neglecting emotional resilience can be significant, leading to increased stress, anxiety, and even chronic health issues.

On a broader scale, cultivating emotional resilience can improve both mental and physical health, reduce the risk of stress-related illnesses, and enhance overall life satisfaction. It can contribute to better sleep, improved focus, and healthier relationships. Resilient individuals are more likely to pursue meaningful goals and engage in activities that bring joy and fulfillment, creating a ripple effect of positivity in their lives and those around them.

As you reflect on the strategies discussed in this chapter, consider how you might integrate them into your daily routine. Think about the small steps you can take to challenge negative thoughts, practice mindfulness, or express gratitude. Emotional resilience is a journey, and every effort you make contributes to building a stronger, more adaptable mind. The path to resilience is unique for everyone, but with consistency and compassion, you can navigate life's ups and downs with greater ease and confidence. What will be your first step towards cultivating emotional resilience today?

Chapter 6

Creating Positive Thought Patterns

Creating positive thought patterns is a journey that involves embracing new ways of thinking and letting go of negativity. This chapter delves into various strategies that can help nurture a more optimistic mindset, which is essential for overall well-being. From simple practices like deep breathing and meditation to more structured approaches like Cognitive Behavioral Therapy (CBT), you'll discover numerous methods to shift your thoughts towards positivity.

Within these pages, you'll learn how to engage in mindfulness practices to stay present, recognize and challenge cognitive distortions, and implement daily affirmations and visualizations. Additionally, the chapter offers practical insights into developing self-compassion and gratitude, fostering a supportive internal environment. By exploring these techniques, you can build a foundation for lasting positive thought patterns, enriching your mental health and enhancing your everyday life.

Strategies for Positive Thinking

Engaging in mindfulness practice can significantly help in observing and detaching from negative thoughts. Mindfulness is the art of being fully present and engaged in the current moment, without judgment. By focusing on the here and now, you can quiet your mind and gain better control over your thoughts. This practice involves simple yet effective techniques such as deep breathing, meditation, and paying close attention to your senses and surroundings. Over time, these methods can train your brain to navigate through negative thinking patterns effortlessly.

One practical way to start incorporating mindfulness into your daily life is through a straightforward meditation exercise. Begin by sitting comfortably in a quiet place, closing your eyes, and taking slow, deep breaths. Focus solely on your breath – the way it feels entering and leaving your body. When distractions or negative thoughts arise, acknowledge them without judgment, and gently bring your focus back to your breathing. Regularly practicing this kind of mindful meditation can help detach from overwhelming negative thoughts, making room for more positive ones.

Mindfulness is not confined to meditation alone. Observing your daily activities with full awareness can also be an effective approach. Whether you are eating, walking, or washing dishes, try to do it mindfully. Pay close attention to every detail and sensation, remaining fully present in the activity. This technique not only improves your focus but also helps you cultivate a sense of calmness and reduces stress, further enhancing your ability to manage negative thoughts constructively.

Developing a present-focused awareness is another essential strategy for shifting attention from negative to positive aspects. Often, our minds tend to ruminate on past regrets or future anxieties, which fosters negative thinking. By grounding ourselves in the present, we can break this cycle and refocus our energy on what is happening right now. Start by recognizing when your mind begins to wander and gently guiding it back to the task at hand.

A useful method to develop present-focused awareness is by practicing mindful breathing throughout the day. Take short breaks to breathe deeply and observe your surroundings. Concentrate on the sights, sounds, and scents around you, allowing yourself to fully experience the present moment. This exercise creates a mental space where negative thoughts lose their power and positive sensations can take over.

In addition, engaging in activities that require a high level of focus can naturally bring your attention to the present. Hobbies such as painting, playing a musical instrument, or gardening demand concentration, helping to ground your awareness in the present moment. These activities not only distract from negative thoughts but also provide a sense of accomplishment, further contributing to a positive mindset.

Practicing non-judgmental observation of one's thoughts is crucial for fostering a positive mental state. It is human nature to judge our thoughts, often harshly, which can lead to increased stress and negative emotions. By learning to observe thoughts without labeling them as good or bad, you can reduce their impact on your emotional well-being. This practice involves acknowledging thoughts as they come, letting them pass like clouds in the sky, without attaching any judgment or emotion to them.

To develop this skill, consider implementing a daily thought journal. Spend a few minutes each day writing down your thoughts as they occur, without analyzing or judging them. Simply record what comes to mind and then let it go. Over time, this practice can help you see your thoughts more objectively, reducing the emotional weight they carry.

Another technique is to use mindful self-compassion. When a negative thought arises, notice it and treat yourself with kindness instead of criticism. Remind yourself that everyone experiences negative thoughts and that it is okay. Offering yourself compassion can mitigate the intensity of negative emotions and promote a more balanced mental state.

Finally, cultivating gratitude and appreciation for the present moment is a powerful way to enhance positive thinking. Gratitude shifts your focus from what you lack to what you have, fostering a positive outlook on life. By regularly acknowledging and appreciating the small joys in your everyday experiences, you can reinforce positive thought patterns and improve your overall well-being.

One effective method to cultivate gratitude is by keeping a gratitude journal. Each day, write down three things you are grateful for. These can range from significant achievements to simple pleasures like a pleasant conversation or a beautiful sunset. Reflecting on these moments can help you appreciate the positives in your life, no matter how small they may seem.

Additionally, expressing gratitude to others can amplify its benefits. Take time to thank the people in your life who make a difference, whether it's a friend, family member, or colleague. Expressing gratitude strengthens relationships and reinforces positive feelings, contributing to a supportive social environment that nurtures a positive mindset.

Cognitive Restructuring

To effectively utilize Cognitive Behavioral Therapy (CBT) techniques for reframing negative thoughts, it's essential to start by identifying cognitive distortions and challenging irrational beliefs through evidence-based reasoning. Cognitive distortions are patterns of thinking that deviate from reality, often leading to negative emotions and behaviors. Common distortions include black-and-white thinking, overgeneralization, and catastrophizing. Recognizing these distortions is the first step towards changing them. By questioning whether our thoughts align with facts or if they are exaggerated, we can start to dismantle their impact on our mental well-being.

Once we've identified cognitive distortions, the next step is to challenge them with evidence-based reasoning. This involves examining the validity of our thoughts and beliefs. For instance, if you find yourself thinking, "I always mess things up," consider whether this is truly accurate. Reflect on past experiences where you did not fail, and recognize those moments as counter-evidence. Additionally, discussing your thoughts with someone you trust can provide an external perspective that may highlight any irrational beliefs you might hold. Evidence-based reasoning helps in creating a more balanced view of ourselves and our capabilities.

After identifying and challenging cognitive distortions, the next task is to create alternative, more balanced interpretations of situations. This approach can significantly reduce negativity bias, which is the tendency to focus more on negative events than positive ones. Imagine you didn't get a promotion at work; instead of thinking, "I'm a failure," you might reframe it as, "This is an opportunity to develop my skills further." By generating multiple interpretations, you can choose the one that promotes balance and positivity, thereby decreasing the emotional impact of negative events.

Creating alternative interpretations also involves understanding the context of a situation. Sometimes, we make snap judgments without considering all factors. Take a moment to think about other possible reasons behind an event. Maybe you weren't promoted because there were no openings, not because you're inadequate. Practicing this kind of balanced thinking regularly will gradually shift your mindset towards a more optimistic outlook. It's essentially training your brain to look for the silver lining in every cloud.

An effective way to reinforce new thought patterns is through implementing positive self-talk and affirmations. Positive self-talk involves replacing negative statements with encouraging ones. For instance, replace "I can't handle this" with "I can find a way through this." This practice boosts your confidence and resilience over time. Similarly, creating personalized affirmations that resonate with you can counteract negative self-perceptions. Statements like "I am capable and strong" can be repeated daily to instill a sense of empowerment and positivity.

Affirmations are particularly useful because they act as mental rehearsals for success. When you continuously tell yourself positive messages, you start believing them, which can lead to improved performance and outcomes. Incorporating affirmations into your daily routine, such as saying them aloud each morning, makes them a habitual part of your life. Over time, these affirmations become ingrained, naturally steering your thoughts in a positive direction. This simple yet powerful tool can have lasting effects on how you perceive and react to life's challenges.

Implementing positive self-talk and affirmations requires consistency. It might feel awkward initially, but persistence is key. Gradually, you will notice a shift in how you respond to adversity. Instead of defaulting to negative thoughts, your mind will lean towards positivity and constructive solutions. Keeping a journal where you record your affirmations and reflect on their impact can be beneficial. Monitoring your progress not only showcases your growth but also provides motivation to continue the practice.

Lastly, monitoring progress and reflecting on cognitive restructuring exercises over time is crucial for sustaining positive thought patterns. Keeping track of your thoughts and behaviors helps you understand what works and what needs adjustment. Regularly reviewing your progress allows you to see tangible improvements, which can be incredibly motivating. Reflection also helps in identifying any recurring negative thoughts that may need further intervention.

Monitoring progress can be done through various methods, such as journaling, using mood tracking apps, or even setting regular check-ins with a therapist. These tools can help you document your journey and measure your achievements. For instance, noting down instances where you've successfully reframed a negative thought into a positive one reinforces the new behavior. Seeing your progress laid out visually can boost your morale and encourage continued effort.

In your reflections, it's important to acknowledge both small and significant victories. Recognize the effort you've put into restructuring your thoughts and celebrate the positive changes, no matter how minor they may seem. This practice fosters a positive feedback loop, making it easier to maintain and build upon your new thought patterns. Regular reflection ensures that you remain mindful of your cognitive habits and stay committed to fostering a positive mindset.

Replacing Negative Thoughts with Positive Ones

One of the first steps in establishing positive thought patterns is to become aware of your current thinking habits through thought monitoring. This involves paying close attention to your thoughts and identifying any recurring negative patterns. You might start by keeping a journal or using a mobile app to record moments when you catch yourself thinking negatively. By doing this consistently, you'll begin to notice trends and common themes in your thoughts.

Recognizing the triggers that lead to negative thinking episodes is equally important. These triggers could be specific situations, people, or even certain times of the day that prompt negative thoughts. For instance, stressful work meetings, interactions with specific individuals, or feeling tired at the end of the day may be common catalysts. Identifying these triggers allows you to anticipate and prepare for them, reducing their power over your mindset.

Tracking the emotional and behavioral outcomes of negative thoughts can provide valuable insights into how they affect your overall well-being. When you dwell on negative thoughts, it often leads to feelings of sadness, anxiety, or anger. These emotions can then influence your behavior, potentially causing you to withdraw from social activities, perform poorly at work, or engage in unhealthy coping mechanisms. By acknowledging these consequences, you'll be more motivated to shift your focus to positive thinking.

An essential part of combatting negative thoughts is recognizing and understanding cognitive distortions. These are irrational thought patterns that skew our perception of reality, such as "all-or-nothing" thinking, overgeneralization, and catastrophizing. By becoming familiar with these distortions, you can start to challenge and reframe them. For example, if you catch yourself thinking, "I always fail at everything," you can counteract it with evidence of past successes to form a more balanced perspective.

Once you've identified your cognitive distortions, it's helpful to examine the recurring negative themes they create. These themes might include self-doubt, fear of failure, or feeling unworthy. Targeting these specific themes can make your efforts to replace negative thoughts more focused and effective. For example, if self-doubt is a recurring theme, you can actively work on building self-confidence through positive affirmations and setting achievable goals.

Furthermore, analyzing the patterns in your negative thoughts can reveal underlying beliefs or assumptions that contribute to your mental state. Perhaps you have an unconscious belief that you're not good enough, which fuels your negative self-talk. Bringing these beliefs to light enables you to question their validity and replace them with more empowering ones. This process of restructuring your core beliefs is crucial for long-term positive change.

As you continue to monitor and analyze your thoughts, it's important to practice self-compassion. It's easy to feel discouraged or frustrated when you notice negative patterns, but remember that everyone experiences them. Treat yourself with kindness and patience as you work through this process. Acknowledge your progress, no matter how small, and remind yourself that change takes time and effort.

Ultimately, increasing your self-awareness through thought monitoring empowers you to take control of your mindset. By consistently practicing these techniques, you can gradually shift your thought patterns towards positivity. This proactive approach not only improves your mental health but also enhances your overall quality of life. Embrace the journey of self-discovery and growth, knowing that each step brings you closer to a more optimistic and fulfilling future.

To further solidify these changes, consider integrating additional supportive practices into your routine. For example, mindfulness meditation can help you stay present and observe your thoughts without judgment, while regular physical activity can boost your mood and reduce stress. Combining these practices with thought monitoring creates a comprehensive strategy for maintaining positive thought patterns.

Daily Affirmations and Visualizations

Daily affirmations and visualizations are powerful tools to help maintain positive thought patterns. These practices can significantly improve mental well-being by instilling positive beliefs and intentions. Engaging in daily affirmations allows individuals to replace negative self-talk with empowering statements, creating a more optimistic mindset over time. It's essential to make this practice consistent, as repetition helps cement these new beliefs into one's subconscious.

Choosing the right affirmations is crucial for their effectiveness. Affirmations should resonate with personal goals and values to have the most significant impact. For example, someone aiming to boost their self-confidence might use affirmations like "I am capable and strong" or "I believe in my abilities." Tailoring affirmations to individual aspirations makes them more meaningful and potent, encouraging personal growth and development.

Repeating affirmations during specific times of the day, such as in the morning or before facing a challenging situation, can be particularly beneficial. Starting the day with positive affirmations sets a constructive tone, while using them before stressful events helps prepare mentally and emotionally. This practice enhances resilience and equips individuals with a positive outlook, which can make handling difficulties smoother and less daunting.

Incorporating visual cues or written reminders can further reinforce the power of positive affirmations. Placing sticky notes with affirmations on mirrors, desks, or other frequently seen places acts as constant encouragement and reinforcement. These visual reminders not only keep the affirmations at the forefront of one's mind but also serve as quick, uplifting boosts throughout the day.

Visualizations are another vital technique in maintaining positive thought patterns. By vividly imagining desired outcomes, individuals can foster a sense of achievement and motivation. Visualization involves creating detailed mental images of achieving specific goals or experiencing positive events. This practice taps into the brain's ability to simulate real experiences, making the envisioned success feel tangible and attainable.

For visualization to be effective, it's important to create clear, vivid images that evoke emotional responses. For instance, if one aims to excel in a presentation, they might visually experience standing confidently in front of an audience, speaking clearly, and receiving positive feedback. The more detailed and emotionally engaging the visualization, the more powerful its impact on one's mindset and behavior.

Combining affirmations with visualizations amplifies the benefits of both practices. Repeating affirmations while visualizing success creates a synergistic effect, reinforcing confidence and belief in one's abilities. This integrated approach can significantly enhance motivation, reduce anxiety, and promote a persistent, positive outlook, even in the face of challenges.

The consistency of these practices plays a crucial role in their effectiveness. Establishing a daily routine that includes affirmations and visualizations ensures that these positive habits become ingrained over time. Committing to a regular schedule, whether it's during morning routines or evening wind-downs, helps maintain focus and reinforces the commitment to fostering positive thought patterns.

Tracking progress and reflecting on the impact of these practices can provide valuable insights and motivation.

Keeping a journal to record the affirmations used, visualizations practiced, and the emotional or behavioral changes observed can highlight improvements and areas that need adjustment. Reflecting on this journey helps maintain momentum and encourages continual growth.

Seeking support from a therapist, coach, or support group can further reinforce these positive changes. Professionals can offer guidance tailored to individual needs, helping refine these practices for maximum benefit. Additionally, sharing experiences and challenges with a supportive community fosters accountability and encouragement, making it easier to maintain these positive habits.

Self-care and self-compassion are fundamental components of nurturing a positive mindset. Prioritizing activities that promote relaxation, joy, and self-expression can significantly enhance mental well-being. Engaging in hobbies, spending time with loved ones, and practicing mindfulness are all ways to recharge and cultivate positivity.

Cultivating self-compassion involves accepting imperfections and mistakes as part of the human experience. Embracing oneself with kindness and understanding, especially during difficult times, helps build resilience and reduces self-criticism. This compassionate approach fosters a healthier, more balanced perspective on challenges and setbacks.

Readers will learn practical strategies, including mindfulness, cognitive restructuring, daily affirmations, and visualizations, to consistently implement positive thought patterns into their lives, fostering lasting positivity and well-being.

Throughout this chapter, we have explored various strategies to establish and maintain positive thought patterns for overall well-being. We've touched on the importance of mindfulness, cognitive restructuring, replacing negative thoughts, and the power of daily affirmations and visualizations. Engaging in these practices can profoundly impact our mental health, fostering a more optimistic and balanced mindset.

At the beginning, we emphasized the significance of mindfulness—a practice that helps us stay present and focused. By observing our thoughts without judgment and grounding ourselves in the here and now, we can reduce the influence of negative thinking patterns. This approach not only calms the mind but also enhances self-awareness, which is crucial for identifying and modifying unhelpful thoughts.

From there, we moved into cognitive restructuring, a technique drawn from Cognitive Behavioral Therapy (CBT). This involves recognizing cognitive distortions and challenging irrational beliefs through evidence-based reasoning. By questioning the validity of our automatic negative thoughts and creating more balanced interpretations, we can shift our perspective towards a more positive outlook. This process requires consistent effort but can lead to long-lasting changes in how we perceive ourselves and the world around us.

Replacing negative thoughts with positive ones is another essential strategy we've covered. Thought monitoring allows us to become aware of recurring negative patterns and their triggers. By understanding these patterns, we can actively work to replace them with positive alternatives. Self-compassion plays a significant role here; treating ourselves with kindness when we encounter negative thoughts can mitigate their impact and promote emotional resilience.

We also delved into the benefits of daily affirmations and visualizations—powerful tools for reinforcing positive thought patterns. Affirmations help us replace negative self-talk with empowering statements, while visualizations enable us to vividly imagine desired outcomes. Combining these practices creates a synergistic effect that enhances confidence, motivation, and overall mental well-being. Consistency is key, as regular engagement with affirmations and visualizations ingrains these positive habits into our daily routine.

However, some readers might be concerned about the feasibility of incorporating these practices into their busy lives. It's important to recognize that even small, incremental changes can make a significant difference. Starting with just a few minutes of mindfulness or one positive affirmation a day can set the foundation for more extensive practices over time. The goal is to integrate these strategies in a way that feels natural and sustainable, gradually building up to a more comprehensive routine.

On a wider scale, establishing positive thought patterns can have profound consequences. Not only does it enhance individual mental health, but it also improves relationships, productivity, and overall quality of life. A positive mindset is contagious; by nurturing our own mental well-being, we can positively influence those around us, creating a ripple effect of positivity and resilience within our communities.

As you reflect on the strategies discussed in this chapter, consider how they might fit into your own life. What small steps can you take today to start cultivating a more positive mindset? Remember, change takes time and effort, but each step forward brings you closer to a healthier, happier future. Embrace the journey of self-discovery and growth, knowing that every moment spent nurturing your mental well-being is a valuable investment in yourself.

Chapter 7

Reducing Anxiety and Stress

Reducing anxiety and stress involves finding strategies that work for you to create a more balanced and peaceful life. We often feel overwhelmed by the demands of daily life, and these feelings can spiral into chronic anxiety or stress if left unaddressed. By focusing on methods like Cognitive Behavioral Therapy (CBT) and mindfulness, we can develop tools to manage our mental health more effectively. Understanding that anxiety and stress are reactions to different triggers helps in identifying which techniques will be most beneficial for specific challenges.

This chapter will delve into various CBT and mindfulness techniques designed to alleviate anxiety and stress. You'll discover how cognitive restructuring can help reframe negative thought patterns that contribute to anxiety. Practical exercises like maintaining thought records will also be discussed, along with behavioral exposure strategies that gradually reduce fear responses. The chapter will explore mindfulness practices such as deep breathing exercises and body scans to help you stay grounded in the present moment. Additionally, tips on incorporating these techniques into your daily routine will provide you with actionable steps to improve your mental well-being.

Understanding Anxiety and Stress

Understanding the root causes and effects of anxiety and stress is essential for addressing these mental health challenges effectively. Anxiety and stress, although often used interchangeably, differ in their experiences and impacts on individuals. Anxiety typically involves feelings of worry, fear, or unease about future events, whereas stress is a response to external pressures or threats. By differentiating between these two, readers can better identify the specific issues they face and seek appropriate strategies to cope.

Recognizing whether one is experiencing anxiety or stress is crucial for targeted treatment. Anxiety often manifests through persistent worries that interfere with daily life, such as concerns about health, work, or relationships. On the other hand, stress results from direct pressures, such as job deadlines or personal conflicts, leading to immediate physical and psychological responses. Understanding these distinctions allows for more personalized interventions, ensuring that individuals receive the most effective support for their unique circumstances.

However, both anxiety and stress share common symptoms that can overlap, making it challenging to distinguish between them. Symptoms of anxiety may include excessive worry, restlessness, and physical symptoms like a racing heart, while stress often leads to irritability, fatigue, and muscle tension. Identifying the specific triggers of each condition can further aid in tailoring treatments, helping individuals manage their mental health more effectively.

The physical and psychological impacts of prolonged anxiety and stress can be profound. Chronic anxiety can lead to severe mental health conditions such as generalized anxiety disorder or panic disorders, affecting an individual's overall well-being. Stress, if not managed, can contribute to significant health issues like hypertension, heart disease, and weakened immune function. Recognizing these potential consequences emphasizes the importance of addressing these issues early on to prevent long-term damage.

Prolonged exposure to stress hormones like cortisol can have detrimental effects on the body. Individuals under constant stress may experience sleep disturbances, digestive problems, and even weight gain. Similarly, the chronic nature of anxiety can lead to persistent fatigue, concentration difficulties, and a constant state of alertness, which exhausts mental and physical resources. These effects illustrate the interconnected nature of mental and physical health, underscoring the need for holistic approaches to treatment.

Discussing the potential long-term consequences of untreated anxiety and stress highlights the urgency of seeking help. Without intervention, the cyclical nature of these conditions can lead to a deterioration in the quality of life, strained relationships, and decreased productivity. Early recognition and treatment can break this cycle, promoting healthier coping mechanisms and reducing the risk of developing more severe health issues.

Early intervention is key to managing anxiety and stress effectively. By addressing these issues before they become entrenched, individuals can develop resilience and learn strategies to navigate life's challenges more successfully. Techniques such as mindfulness practices and cognitive-behavioral therapy provide tools to manage symptoms and improve overall well-being, demonstrating the benefits of proactive mental health care.

CBT Methods for Anxiety Management

When dealing with anxiety, it is crucial to recognize and reframe negative thoughts that often exacerbate stress. One effective evidence-based technique to achieve this is cognitive restructuring. This method empowers individuals to challenge irrational thoughts contributing to their anxiety, ultimately replacing them with more balanced and rational beliefs.

Cognitive restructuring starts by identifying distorted thinking patterns such as all-or-nothing thinking, overgeneralization, or catastrophizing. For example, someone might believe, "I failed at my presentation, so I'm a complete failure." By challenging this thought, one could consider other successful presentations they've done, reframing the belief to, "This presentation didn't go as planned, but I have done well in the past and can improve next time." This shift in perspective can significantly alleviate feelings of anxiety associated with perceived failures.

Practical examples help illustrate this process. Imagine Sarah, who feels anxious before social gatherings because she thinks people will judge her negatively. She identifies this automatic thought and examines the evidence: While she has had some negative experiences, most interactions have been positive or neutral. By focusing on this balanced view, Sarah can replace her original thought with something like, "I'm not perfect, but most people enjoy my company." Practical exercises like maintaining thought records can further aid in practicing and mastering cognitive restructuring techniques.

Another critical technique in combating anxiety is behavioral exposure. This involves gradually exposing oneself to anxiety-inducing situations in a controlled manner. The goal is to build resilience and decrease fear responses over time. For instance, if public speaking triggers anxiety, one might start by speaking in front of a small group and gradually increase the audience size as comfort grows.

Behavioral exposure is essential because it breaks the cycle of avoidance, which often perpetuates anxiety. Avoidance behaviors can provide short-term relief, but they prevent individuals from learning that the feared situation may not be as threatening as imagined. Over time, repeated exposure helps retrain the brain to respond with less fear and anxiety.

A systematic approach to exposure, known as systematic desensitization, can be particularly effective. This technique combines gradual exposure with relaxation exercises to reduce fear and avoidant behaviors. For example, someone afraid of flying might start by visualizing being on a plane while practicing deep breathing. Gradually, they might progress to visiting an airport, sitting in a stationary plane, and eventually taking a short flight. Each step should be manageable and paired with relaxation strategies to ensure a gradual reduction in anxiety.

Mindfulness Methods for Stress Relief

Mindfulness practices are powerful tools for managing stress and promoting mental clarity. One of the primary goals of mindfulness is to cultivate an awareness of the present moment. In our fast-paced lives, it's easy to get caught up in worries about the future or regrets about the past. However, by focusing on the here and now, we can significantly alleviate stress. Mindfulness encourages us to tune into our current experience, be it the sensations in our body or the thoughts passing through our mind, without any judgment. This practice helps us become more grounded and less reactive to external pressures.

Awareness of the present moment involves paying attention to simple activities we might normally overlook. For instance, when you are washing dishes, notice the temperature of the water, the scent of the soap, and the feeling of the dishes in your hands. By doing this, you anchor yourself in the present moment rather than letting your mind wander to other concerns. This shift in focus can reduce anxiety levels and provide a welcome break from constant mental chatter. It may seem small, but these moments of mindful awareness add up, creating a cumulative effect that fosters greater peace and calm.

Incorporating mindfulness into daily routines doesn't need to be complicated. Even setting aside just five minutes a day to focus on your breathing or observe your surroundings can make a significant difference. The key is consistency and making these practices a part of your daily life. As you become more familiar with mindfulness, you'll likely find that you're better able to manage stress and maintain mental clarity even in challenging situations. By focusing on the present, we're not only reducing stress but also enhancing our overall well-being.

Another effective mindfulness technique to combat stress is deep breathing exercises. Deep breathing helps activate the body's relaxation response, which counteracts the stress response. When we are stressed, our breathing becomes shallow and rapid. By consciously slowing down our breath and taking deeper inhalations and exhalations, we signal to our body that it is time to relax. This can provide immediate relief from stress and anxiety.

One simple exercise is to sit comfortably, close your eyes, and take a deep breath in through your nose for a count of four. Hold your breath for a count of four, then slowly exhale through your mouth for a count of eight. Repeating this cycle several times can help to calm the nervous system and bring a sense of tranquility. This practice can be done anywhere, whether you're at home, at work, or even in a public place like a park or bus stop.

Deep breathing doesn't just provide short-term relief. Over time, consistent practice can lead to longer-lasting changes in how we respond to stressors. By regularly engaging in deep breathing, we teach our bodies to stay calmer under pressure, improving our resilience against everyday stress. Integrating deep breathing exercises into your routine can thus serve as a reliable tool for maintaining emotional balance and reducing stress.

Acceptance and non-judgment are integral components of mindfulness. Rather than reacting to difficult emotions or thoughts, mindfulness encourages us to observe them without judgment. This helps create a space where we can experience our feelings without becoming overwhelmed by them. Acceptance means recognizing that it's okay to have negative thoughts or feelings; they are a normal part of human experience. By adopting a non-reactive stance, we can reduce the intensity of our stress and anxiety.

For example, if you're feeling stressed about an upcoming deadline, instead of allowing the stress to consume you, acknowledge the feeling: "I am feeling anxious right now." Just noting this emotion without attaching a story to it can diminish its power over you. This doesn't mean ignoring the issue, but rather approaching it with a clearer, calmer mind. Accepting your emotions as they come allows for a greater sense of peace and control.

Practicing non-judgment also extends to how we view ourselves and our thoughts. Often, we judge ourselves harshly for having certain thoughts or feelings, which can amplify stress. By viewing our mental experiences with compassion and without criticism, we foster a kinder relationship with ourselves. This approach not only lowers stress but also enhances overall mental wellness.

Acceptance, as part of mindfulness, plays a crucial role in decreasing rumination and increasing well-being. Rumination, or repeatedly thinking about distressing events, is a common response to stress but often exacerbates anxiety and depression. Mindfulness teaches us to accept our thoughts and feelings without getting stuck in them, breaking the cycle of rumination.

By practicing acceptance, we learn to let go of the constant need to fix or change our experiences. For instance, if you're repeatedly thinking about a past mistake, mindfulness encourages you to acknowledge that thought and then gently redirect your focus back to the present moment. This process helps prevent you from spiraling into negative thinking patterns and promotes a more balanced emotional state.

Regular mindfulness practice can lead to lasting improvements in mental health. Studies have shown that individuals who consistently practice mindfulness experience increased levels of well-being, reduced symptoms of stress and anxiety, and greater emotional regulation. By embracing acceptance and non-judgment, these benefits become more accessible, encouraging sustained practice and ongoing personal growth.

Exercises to Incorporate into Daily Routine

To effectively reduce anxiety and stress, integrating Cognitive Behavioral Therapy (CBT) and mindfulness techniques into everyday life is essential. One of the most practical ways to do this is through daily thought monitoring. This practice involves tracking your thoughts throughout the day and identifying negative patterns that contribute to stress and anxiety. By recognizing these patterns, you can begin to challenge and reframe them in a more positive light.

Daily thought monitoring requires a dedicated effort and a bit of patience. Start by setting aside specific times during the day to reflect on your thoughts. Morning, midday, and evening are good checkpoints. During these moments, jot down any negative or anxious thoughts. Once you've identified these thoughts, ask yourself whether they are rational or based on assumptions and fears. Challenging these thoughts involves looking for evidence that contradicts them and considering alternative perspectives that are more balanced and less distressing.

To make this practice more structured, consider using a thought diary. A thought diary helps you systematically record your thoughts, identify cognitive distortions, and develop healthier thinking patterns. For instance, if you find yourself thinking, "I always mess things up," you can challenge this by noting instances where you have succeeded. Over time, this practice can help reduce the automaticity of negative thinking and promote a more positive and relaxed mindset.

Journaling prompts can be a powerful tool for self-reflection and cognitive awareness. These prompts guide you to explore your thoughts and feelings deeply, providing insights that can lead to personal growth and emotional resilience. Journaling about your experiences helps to externalize your thoughts, making it easier to analyze and understand them.

Begin with simple prompts like, "What are three things I am grateful for today?" or "Describe a recent situation where I felt anxious and how I handled it." Such prompts encourage you to focus on the positive aspects of your day and assess how you respond to challenges. Regularly engaging in this practice can enhance your ability to manage stress and anxiety by improving your self-awareness and coping skills.

Another effective journaling prompt is to reflect on your triggers. Understanding what causes your anxiety can help you develop strategies to mitigate these triggers. Write about a recent event that caused stress, describing your immediate thoughts and physical reactions. Then, consider how you might approach similar situations differently in the future. This process of reflection and planning can build your confidence and reduce anxiety over time.

Incorporating mindful moments into your daily routine is another powerful technique for managing stress. Mindfulness exercises can be brief and easily integrated into even the busiest schedules. Activities such as deep breathing, body scans, or a few minutes of quiet meditation can significantly enhance present-moment awareness and reduce stress.

Start with a simple deep-breathing exercise: inhale deeply through your nose to a count of four, hold for a count of four, and exhale slowly through your mouth to a count of six. Repeat this several times whenever you feel overwhelmed. This practice not only calms your nervous system but also brings your focus back to the present moment, breaking the cycle of worry and tension.

Another mindful exercise is the body scan. Take a few minutes to sit quietly and mentally scan your body from head to toe, noticing any areas of tension without trying to change anything. This practice helps you become more attuned to your body's signals and can serve as an early warning system for rising stress levels. Integrating these small, mindful pauses throughout your day can create a sense of balance and calm, helping you navigate stressful situations with greater ease.

Finally, the adaptability of mindfulness practices means they can be utilized in various settings, encouraging consistent use. Whether you're at home, at work, or commuting, there's always an opportunity to practice mindfulness. For example, while waiting in line, instead of reaching for your phone, take a moment to observe your surroundings, notice your breath, and ground yourself in the present.

At work, you can incorporate mindful moments by taking short breaks to stretch, breathe, or simply gaze out the window. These mini-breaks can refresh your mind and reduce the cumulative stress of a busy day. Even during meetings or conversations, practicing active listening—fully focusing on the speaker without judgment—can be a form of mindfulness, fostering better connections and reducing interpersonal stress.

The beauty of mindfulness is its flexibility. It's not limited to formal meditation sessions; rather, it's a way of being that can permeate all aspects of life. The more you integrate mindfulness into your daily activities, the more natural it becomes, ultimately leading to sustained stress reduction and a more balanced, peaceful life.

Readers will have a toolbox of practical exercises to incorporate CBT and mindfulness into their daily routines, promoting sustained stress management and emotional well-being.

Throughout this chapter, we have explored the ins and outs of anxiety and stress, shedding light on their differences and commonalities. By understanding these mental health challenges, we have laid a foundation to address them more effectively. We have delved into Cognitive Behavioral Therapy (CBT) techniques like cognitive restructuring and behavioral exposure, which help reshape our thoughts and reactions. Additionally, mindfulness practices such as deep breathing and present-moment awareness offer powerful tools to manage stress.

Revisiting our initial focus, it is clear that recognizing whether you are dealing with anxiety or stress is key. This differentiation allows for tailored interventions, ensuring you get the most effective support. Our position emphasizes using CBT to tackle negative thought patterns and mindfulness to stay grounded in the present. Combining these techniques creates a robust approach to managing both anxiety and stress.

Some readers might worry about the challenges of integrating these methods into daily life. It is natural to feel apprehensive when forming new habits. However, it is important to remember that small, consistent steps can lead to significant change over time. Daily thought monitoring, mindful moments, and journaling prompts are all manageable ways to incorporate these practices into your routine.

The broader consequences of not addressing anxiety and stress are profound. Unmanaged anxiety can lead to severe disorders, while chronic stress can contribute to serious health problems like heart disease. Early intervention not only improves current well-being but also prevents long-term health issues.

As we conclude, consider how these techniques can fit into your life. Imagine the cumulative effect of daily mindfulness practice or the shift in perspective from restructured thoughts. These small changes can lead to a more balanced, peaceful existence. Remember, the journey to better mental health is ongoing, and each step you take brings you closer to a calmer, happier life.

Chapter 8

Achieving Lasting Happiness and Inner Peace

Achieving lasting happiness and inner peace is a transformative journey that goes beyond momentary pleasures. The fleeting joy from buying a new gadget or enjoying a meal often dissipates quickly, leaving us chasing the next temporary fix. In contrast, genuine happiness comes from within, rooted in deeper contentment and fulfillment. Understanding this core difference sets the foundation for cultivating long-term mental well-being. This chapter delves into sustained happiness, exploring how internal sources, rather than external circumstances, can lead to a more stable and enduring sense of satisfaction.

Throughout this chapter, you'll learn practical strategies and habits designed to foster a positive mental state amidst life's ups and downs. We will explore the concept of viewing happiness as a continuous journey rather than a one-time achievement, emphasizing the importance of finding joy in the process rather than just in milestones. The discussion will also cover how meaningful activities aligned with our core values can add a profound sense of purpose and fulfillment. By incorporating mindfulness practices, gratitude, and building strong social connections, this chapter aims to equip you with tools to maintain positive mental health, no matter the challenges you face.

Defining Lasting Happiness

Understanding the difference between lasting happiness and temporary satisfaction is crucial for achieving true inner peace. Temporary satisfaction often arises from short-lived pleasures, such as buying a new gadget or enjoying a delicious meal. These moments provide immediate joy but quickly fade, leaving a void that prompts the search for the next quick fix. In contrast, lasting happiness involves a deeper sense of contentment and fulfillment that isn't dependent on fleeting external circumstances.

Lasting happiness stems from internal sources and is characterized by a steady state of well-being. It's cultivated through sustained practices and attitudes that enhance one's overall quality of life. This kind of happiness doesn't waver with life's ups and downs because it's rooted in deeper values and long-term goals. While the excitement from temporary pleasures can be intense, it tends to diminish rapidly, highlighting the need for a more enduring form of happiness.

Recognizing that happiness is a continuous journey rather than a destination is another essential aspect to understand. Many people fall into the trap of thinking they'll be happy once they achieve certain milestones like getting a promotion, buying a house, or reaching retirement. However, these are not permanent solutions but rather temporary highs. True happiness is about finding joy in the process, not just the end result.

Viewing happiness as a journey encourages continuous personal growth and adaptation. Life will always have its set of challenges and changes, and recognizing this helps us stay grounded and resilient. Instead of waiting for perfect conditions to be happy, we learn to find contentment in our daily lives. This perspective shifts the focus from outside achievements to internal harmony, making it easier to maintain a positive mental state regardless of circumstances.

Finding purpose and meaning in life plays a significant role in achieving lasting happiness. When we engage in activities that reflect our core values and passions, we experience a sense of fulfillment that transcends momentary pleasure. Purpose gives our lives direction and helps us navigate through difficult times with greater ease and optimism.

Having a sense of purpose connects us to something larger than ourselves, enhancing our emotional and psychological well-being. Whether it's through a career, relationships, hobbies, or community service, purposeful engagement brings a profound sense of satisfaction. It aligns our actions with our beliefs, creating congruence and reducing internal conflict, which contributes significantly to lasting happiness.

Appreciating the present moment and finding joy in small everyday experiences is a powerful way to cultivate lasting happiness. Often, we overlook the simple pleasures in life as we rush towards bigger goals. However, taking time to savor daily moments can greatly enhance our overall sense of well-being.

Mindfulness practices, like deep breathing and meditation, can help us become more aware of the present, allowing us to fully experience each moment without distraction. This heightened awareness makes even mundane tasks feel more meaningful and enjoyable. For instance, savoring a cup of coffee in the morning or enjoying a walk in the park can provide immense joy when we are fully present.

Cultivating gratitude is a practical guideline for appreciating the present moment. By regularly reflecting on things we're thankful for, we shift our focus away from what we lack and towards what we have. Writing a daily gratitude journal can help reinforce this habit, making it easier to find joy in everyday experiences. Over time, this practice can significantly boost our mood and contribute to lasting happiness.

Building connections with others also plays a critical role in achieving lasting happiness. Close relationships with family and friends provide emotional support and create a sense of belonging. Engaging in deeper conversations and spending quality time with loved ones can strengthen these bonds and enrich our lives.

Meaningful social interactions encourage feelings of empathy, compassion, and understanding. They remind us that we are part of a greater community, reducing the sense of isolation that often accompanies stress and anxiety. Sharing our joys and challenges with others makes our experiences more vivid and helps build a more supportive network, adding layers to our happiness.

Pursuing passions and engaging in activities that align with personal values is another way to foster lasting happiness. When we immerse ourselves in pursuits that genuinely interest us, we enter a state of flow where time seems to stand still. This deep engagement not only brings immediate satisfaction but also enhances our skills and personal growth over time.

Whether it's painting, playing a musical instrument, or gardening, these activities provide an outlet for creativity and self-expression. They help us connect with our inner selves and offer a break from daily stressors. Finding and nurturing these interests can significantly contribute to a sustained sense of happiness and fulfillment.

Role of Self-Awareness in Achieving Peace

Self-awareness is a powerful tool in nurturing inner peace and tranquility. By practicing introspection and self-reflection, individuals can enhance their understanding of their inner thoughts and gain deeper insights into their motivations and behaviors. Taking time to reflect on daily experiences, journaling about personal feelings, or simply sitting quietly with one's thoughts allows for a better grasp of the mental and emotional states that drive one's actions. This practice fosters a heightened level of awareness, enabling individuals to discern patterns and triggers that may cause unrest or discomfort.

Recognizing and managing emotions effectively is another crucial aspect of achieving inner peace. Emotions are an integral part of human experience, and learning to identify and understand them can lead to a sense of calm and stability. When individuals can name their emotions, whether it's anger, sadness, joy, or frustration, they gain power over them instead of being controlled by them. Techniques such as deep breathing, meditation, or seeking support from loved ones or professionals can aid in processing emotions healthily. Through this understanding, one can respond to situations more mindfully rather than reacting impulsively, thereby maintaining a balanced and peaceful state of mind.

Embracing flaws and limitations plays a significant role in fostering self-compassion and reducing inner turmoil. Perfection is an unattainable goal, and striving for it often leads to undue stress and self-criticism. Acknowledging personal imperfections allows for a kinder and more forgiving attitude toward oneself. When individuals accept their limitations, they can focus on growth and improvement rather than dwelling on shortcomings. This self-compassionate approach reduces internal conflict and promotes a more harmonious inner life. By viewing mistakes as opportunities for learning rather than failures, one can maintain a positive and tranquil mindset.

Engaging in mindfulness practices is essential for promoting presence and awareness, further aiding in the reduction of internal conflicts and the promotion of peace. Mindfulness involves staying present in the moment and fully experiencing it without judgment. Practices such as mindful breathing, body scans, or mindful eating help anchor individuals in the here and now, preventing the mind from wandering to past regrets or future anxieties. This presence enables a clearer understanding of one's current state, facilitating a more profound connection with inner thoughts and feelings. As mindfulness becomes a regular habit, it cultivates a continuous sense of peace and balance.

Mindful reflection through introspection creates a space for continuous growth and self-discovery. Regularly setting aside moments to introspect allows individuals to evaluate their goals, desires, and values. This ongoing process helps in aligning actions with true intentions, ensuring that life choices resonate deeply within. Whether it's through meditation, prayer, or solitary walks, creating these moments of self-reflection enhances self-awareness and nurtures a peaceful inner landscape.

Embracing emotional intelligence by recognizing and managing emotions also contributes to long-term well-being. Developing skills to navigate complex emotional landscapes builds resilience and adaptability. It involves not only understanding one's emotions but also empathizing with others. This empathy fosters better interpersonal relationships and reduces conflicts both internally and externally. Techniques like cognitive-behavioral strategies or guided visualization can be employed to strengthen emotional intelligence, leading to a calmer and more composed demeanor in various life situations.

Accepting and embracing imperfections fosters a culture of self-love and compassion. This acceptance is not about complacency but about recognizing humanity's inherent imperfection. Instead of harshly judging oneself for perceived failings, reframe these moments as valuable lessons. Cultivating a mindset that welcomes flaws with kindness diminishes the self-imposed pressure to be perfect, opening up avenues for genuine happiness and peace. Positive affirmations, supportive social circles, and professional counseling can assist in reinforcing this compassionate perspective.

Cultivating mindfulness through consistent practice fortifies the foundation of inner peace. Regular engagement in activities that promote mindfulness ensures sustained benefits over time. Yoga, tai chi, or even mindful walking are practical ways to integrate mindfulness into daily routines. These practices encourage a state of flow where the mind and body are harmoniously synchronized, enhancing overall well-being. Making time for these practices each day can significantly improve mental clarity and emotional stability, contributing to an enduring sense of tranquility.

Living in the moment by letting go of past regrets and future anxieties further cements inner peace. Dwelling in the past or fretting about the future often leads to unnecessary stress and anxiety. By focusing on the present, individuals can appreciate the beauty and opportunities that exist in the now. This shift in perspective requires conscious effort and practice but yields immense rewards. Activities such as gratitude journaling or engaging fully in creative pursuits help anchor the mind in the present, fostering a lasting sense of contentment and calm.

Sustaining Positive Mental Health Habits

Maintaining positive mental health and well-being is a continuous journey that involves adopting key habits and behaviors. One foundational practice is engaging in regular physical activity, which not only boosts physical health but also significantly enhances mental wellness. Exercise releases endorphins, the body's natural mood lifters, which can help alleviate symptoms of depression and anxiety. Additionally, physical activity improves brain function, supports better sleep, and reduces stress levels, promoting overall mental stability. Starting with simple activities such as daily walks or joining a local gym can lay the groundwork for more intense exercise routines, fostering long-term mental health benefits.

A balanced diet is equally crucial in supporting ongoing mental wellness. Consuming a variety of nutrient-rich foods provides the necessary vitamins and minerals to maintain brain health and stable energy levels throughout the day. Incorporating fruits, vegetables, lean proteins, and whole grains into daily meals can enhance cognitive function and improve mood. Staying hydrated by drinking plenty of water, while limiting caffeine and alcohol, further contributes to a balanced state of mind. Making mindful dietary choices can create a positive impact on mental well-being, helping individuals feel healthier and more alert.

Prioritizing adequate rest completes this triad of healthy lifestyle choices. Ensuring sufficient rest allows the body and mind to recover from daily stresses, enhancing overall resilience. Aim for seven to nine hours of quality sleep each night, and consider incorporating short breaks during the day to recharge. Regular rest periods not only prevent burnout but also improve emotional regulation and cognitive performance. By prioritizing physical activity, a balanced diet, and adequate rest, individuals can build a strong foundation for sustained mental wellness (National Institutes of Health, 2022).

Establishing a consistent sleep routine is another vital strategy for mental well-being. Regular sleep patterns regulate the body's internal clock, improving both the quantity and quality of sleep. Going to bed and waking up at the same time each day helps reinforce these cycles, leading to better mood regulation and enhanced cognitive function. Creating a bedtime ritual, such as reading a book or taking a warm bath, signals to the body that it is time to wind down, making it easier to fall asleep.

The environment in which one sleeps also plays a significant role in maintaining a healthy sleep routine. Keeping the bedroom cool, dark, and free from distractions can encourage deeper, more restorative sleep. Reducing exposure to screens and electronic devices before bedtime helps minimize blue light interference, which can disrupt the production of melatonin, a hormone that regulates sleep. Instead, engage in relaxing activities that promote a sense of calm and prepare the mind for restful sleep.

Sticking to a sleep schedule and creating a conducive sleep environment can significantly impact one's ability to manage stress and emotions effectively. Proper sleep hygiene strengthens immune function, enhances brain performance, and improves overall mood, contributing to a stable and resilient mental state. With consistent efforts to maintain healthy sleep habits, individuals can experience lasting improvements in their mental and emotional well-being (National Institute of Mental Health, 2024).

Incorporating relaxation practices is essential for alleviating stress and promoting inner peace. Techniques like deep breathing, meditation, and mindfulness exercises can help manage stress levels and foster a sense of calm. Deep breathing exercises, for instance, activate the body's relaxation response, counteracting the effects of stress and lowering heart rate. Practicing deep breaths for just a few minutes daily can reduce anxiety and increase clarity of thought.

Meditation is another effective relaxation practice that encourages mindfulness and presence. By focusing on the breath and being aware of the present moment, meditation helps quiet the mind and diminish the impact of negative thoughts. Regular meditation practice has been shown to decrease symptoms of depression, improve emotional regulation, and enhance overall mental well-being. Guided meditation sessions or apps can be excellent resources for beginners looking to establish a meditation routine.

Furthermore, mindfulness exercises can be seamlessly integrated into daily life to manage stress. Simple mindfulness activities, such as mindful eating or walking, involve paying attention to sensory experiences without judgment. This heightened awareness helps shift focus away from stressful thoughts and fosters a sense of gratitude and contentment. By incorporating various relaxation techniques into daily routines, individuals can combat stress and cultivate a peaceful state of mind.

Another critical aspect of maintaining mental health resilience is building a strong support network. Surrounding oneself with supportive friends, family, and communities provides practical and emotional assistance during challenging times. Sharing experiences and feelings with trusted individuals can offer comfort, reduce feelings of isolation, and enhance emotional well-being. Having a reliable support system also encourages open communication and fosters a sense of belonging.

Seeking professional help when needed is an integral component of mental health care. Licensed therapists, counselors, and mental health professionals possess the expertise to guide individuals through complex emotional issues and offer evidence-based strategies for coping. Therapy can provide a safe space to explore personal challenges, develop healthier thought patterns, and acquire tools for managing stress and anxiety. Engaging in regular therapy sessions can reinforce positive mental health habits and promote long-term resilience.

Peer support groups are another valuable resource for those seeking connection and understanding. Participating in group therapy or support meetings can facilitate a sense of solidarity among individuals facing similar struggles. The shared experiences within these groups create an environment of mutual encouragement, reducing stigma and empowering participants to take proactive steps towards mental wellness. By actively engaging in support networks and professional services, individuals can bolster their mental health and achieve inner peace (National Institute of Mental Health, 2024).

Future Steps for Continuous Improvement

Establishing realistic and achievable goals is fundamental in the journey toward lasting happiness and inner peace. When we set attainable objectives, we create a clear path that motivates us to move forward. These goals provide a sense of purpose and direction, helping us navigate through life's challenges with more certainty and determination. Realistic goals ensure that our efforts are focused and manageable, reducing the likelihood of feeling overwhelmed and disheartened by unattainable aspirations.

One effective strategy for setting realistic goals involves breaking them down into smaller, actionable steps. For example, if your overarching goal is to improve mental well-being, you might start by committing to daily mindfulness exercises or weekly therapy sessions. Smaller milestones offer frequent opportunities for success, boosting your motivation and reinforcing positive behavior. This approach also allows you to adjust your course as needed, ensuring steady progress regardless of minor setbacks.

Moreover, establishing realistic goals can foster a stronger sense of self-efficacy. As you achieve each milestone, no matter how small, you build confidence in your ability to make meaningful changes in your life. This growing belief in your capabilities can be incredibly empowering, encouraging you to tackle more significant challenges with resilience and optimism. By consistently setting and achieving realistic goals, you lay a solid foundation for continued growth and long-term mental well-being.

Monitoring personal growth and celebrating small victories play crucial roles in maintaining motivation and fostering improvement. Regularly assessing your progress allows you to recognize the strides you have made, providing a tangible reminder of your abilities and the effectiveness of your strategies. Documenting these achievements can be as simple as keeping a journal or using a habit-tracking app, which offers visual evidence of your growth over time.

Celebrating small victories, such as completing a week of daily exercise or successfully managing a stressful situation, reinforces positive behavior and encourages consistency. These celebrations do not need to be grand; they can be modest rewards like treating yourself to a favorite book or enjoying a relaxing activity. Acknowledging these wins helps maintain enthusiasm and reduces the risk of burnout by reminding you of your progress and the benefits of your efforts.

Additionally, sharing your achievements with supportive friends or family members can amplify the positive impact of celebrating small victories. Positive reinforcement from others validates your experiences and strengthens social bonds, contributing to a robust support network. This communal aspect of celebration can provide additional motivation, as knowing that others are rooting for your success can inspire you to keep pushing forward on your journey to mental well-being.

Being open to adapting strategies and approaches is essential for ongoing mental health progression. Life is dynamic, and what works for you at one point may not be as effective later. Flexibility in your methods allows you to respond to changing circumstances and evolving needs. This adaptability ensures that your strategies remain relevant and practical, promoting sustained mental health improvements.

For instance, you might find that while meditation was highly beneficial during a particularly stressful period, you now require more physical activity to manage your current stress levels effectively. By being willing to experiment with different techniques, you can discover new methods that better suit your evolving situation and continue to support your mental well-being. This openness to change prevents stagnation and keeps your self-improvement efforts fresh and effective.

Embracing flexibility also means being kind to yourself when adjustments are necessary. It is important to view changes in your approach not as failures but as part of a dynamic process of self-discovery and growth. This mindset fosters resilience, as it encourages you to learn from your experiences and continuously refine your strategies. By staying adaptable, you ensure that your journey toward lasting happiness and inner peace remains sustainable and responsive to your unique needs.

Engaging in continual learning and self-discovery is a powerful way to expand perspectives and enhance mental resilience. Lifelong learning opens doors to new ideas, skills, and ways of thinking that can enrich your life and bolster your mental strength. Whether through formal education, reading, workshops, or exploring new hobbies, the pursuit of knowledge cultivates curiosity and a growth mindset.

Continuous learning also equips you with tools and insights to better understand yourself and the world around you. For example, studying psychological principles can provide deeper insights into your behaviors and thought patterns, enabling you to develop more effective coping mechanisms. This increased self-awareness can lead to more mindful decisions and improved emotional regulation, both of which contribute to overall mental well-being.

By following these strategies and incorporating the lessons learned, readers can work towards achieving sustainable happiness and inner peace in their lives.

As we draw this chapter to a close, it's important to remember the key points we've discussed about lasting happiness and inner peace. We've explored the difference between fleeting pleasures and deeper contentment, emphasizing that true happiness stems from within and is nurtured by consistent practices and attitudes.

Revisiting our earlier thoughts, we underscored that happiness should be viewed as an ongoing journey rather than a final destination. This perspective encourages us to find joy in everyday processes rather than waiting for big milestones. Recognizing that life will always present challenges, adapting and growing through these experiences helps maintain a positive and resilient mindset.

One crucial element we've noted is the significance of purpose and meaning. Engaging in activities that align with our core values fosters a sense of fulfillment that goes beyond temporary pleasure. By connecting our actions with deeper beliefs, we create harmony within ourselves, contributing significantly to long-term happiness.

It's also worth mentioning how mindfulness plays a pivotal role in appreciating the present moment. Simple practices like deep breathing and meditation help us savor daily experiences and reduce anxieties about the past or future. Cultivating gratitude and being present amplifies our well-being, making even ordinary moments more meaningful.

Building strong connections with others further enhances our happiness. Relationships provide emotional support and a sense of belonging, reminding us that we are part of a larger community. These bonds enrich our lives and help us navigate through both joys and difficulties.

In pursuing passions and interests, we find another path to lasting happiness. Immersing ourselves in activities that resonate deeply with us not only brings immediate joy but also promotes personal growth over time.

As you reflect on these strategies, consider what resonates most with your own journey. Everyone's path to happiness and inner peace looks different, and it's essential to find what truly works for you. Implementing these practical habits and staying open to adaptation ensures that your efforts are sustainable and responsive to your evolving needs.

On a broader scale, embracing these principles can lead to a more compassionate and harmonious society. As individuals cultivate their happiness and inner peace, they contribute positively to their communities, fostering environments that support collective well-being.

As you move forward, keep these insights in mind and continue exploring ways to nurture your happiness and inner peace. Remember, this journey is ongoing, filled with opportunities for growth and self-discovery. Stay curious, stay open, and embrace each step with resilience and optimism.

References

Haybron, D. (2011, July). *Happiness (Stanford Encyclopedia of Philosophy)*. Stanford.edu . https://plato.stanford.edu/entries/happiness/

Meditation and Mindfulness: What You Need To Know. NCCIH. (n.d.). https://

communitydev.csusm.edu/mod/url/view.php?id=89307&redirect=1

National Institute of Mental Health. (2024, February). *Caring for your Mental Health. National Institute of Mental Health.* https://www.nimh.nih.gov/health/topics/caring-for-your-mental-health

National Institutes of Health. (2022, August). *Emotional wellness toolkit. National Institutes of Health (NIH).* https://www.nih.gov/health-information/emotional-wellness-toolkit

The Pursuit of Happiness – Psychology. opentext.wsu.edu . (n.d.). https://opentext.wsu.edu/psych105nusbaum/chapter/the-pursuit-of-happiness/

www.ingramcontent.com/pod-product-compliance
Lightning Source LLC
Chambersburg PA
CBHW071830210526
45479CB00001B/71